THINK... ...SERIES

THIRD EDITION
Jonas F. Soltis, *Editor*

The rev... ...sed Third Edition of this series bu... ...the
stre...gth... of the p...ed... Written in clear and conc... style,
thes...   ...epth... to...   ...hers. Each oth...rs
usef...   ...ght-provoking insig... ...ly
prac...   ...ts a needed ...e-
twee...   ...g,
lear...   ...le
read

APPROACHES
=== TO ===
TEACHING

THIRD EDITION

GARY D FENSTERMACHER
University of Michigan

JONAS F. SOLTIS
Teachers College, Columbia University

Teachers College, Columbia University
New York and London

Published by Teachers College Press, 1234 Amsterdam Avenue, New York, NY 10027

Library of Congress Cataloging-in-Publication Data

Fenstermacher, Gary D.
  Approaches to teaching / Gary D Fenstermacher, Jonas F. Soltis.—
3rd ed.
    p.   cm. — (Thinking about education series)
  Includes bibliographical references (p.   ).
  ISBN 0-8077-3809-3 (pbk. : alk. paper)
    1. Teaching. 2. Effective teaching. 3. Case method. 4. Education—
Philosophy.   I. Soltis, Jonas F.   II. Title.   III. Series
LB1025.3. F46   1998
371.102—ddc21   98-44279

Contents

Acknowledgments

We would like to thank a number of institutions and individuals that have contributed in different ways to the first writing of this book and to the completion of the subsequent editions. Some have been mentioned in earlier books in the series. They include Tom Rotell, Lois Patton, and Susan Liddicoat of Teachers College Press. To that list we add and thank for their sustained efforts on the series' behalf Carole Saltz, who joined the Press as director just as the first edition of the series got underway, and Sarah Biondello, both of whom supported and encouraged the rewriting of the second edition; Sandra Pak, Bronwyn Britt, and Peter Sieger, who contributed production expertise; and Mel Berk, who has helped us reach a broad audience. In fact, everyone at the Press has been most supportive. Nancy Soltis also deserves special recognition for her patience, love, and understanding through what sometimes seemed to be the endless process of the nonstop writing of five books and for the retyping of changes for the second edition. Virginia Richardson, forgiving spouse of Gary, offered him the wise counsel and deep insight of a superb colleague and marvelous friend. David Berliner and Lee Shulman shared their scholarship and friendship. Karl Hostetler ably served as research assistant and jack-of-all-trades to the first edition. He and the following people contributed ideas for the cases and disputes included in chapter 7: Tim Counihan, Susan Moyers, Barbara Reynolds, Janet Skupien, and Michael Weinstock. In the second edition, Susan Soltis gave us a perceptive description of the therapist teacher at work. Fran Simon provided word-processing skills for the first edition. And last but not least we thank our own teachers, students, and colleagues, who have encouraged us to think deeply about teaching. Their prodding also resulted in our addition of a new, reflective chapter in this third edition.

A Note to the Student
and Instructor

This book was designed so that it could be used in a number of ways to suit the purposes and style of the instructor. All or any lesser combination of the five texts in this series can be used together in a basic foundations course. This book or any of the others in this series also can be used singly as the primary text for a full course on its topic, as supplemental reading, or as a source for cases and dialogues to stimulate class discussion.

We wrote this book with a style and tone that assumes it will be assigned early in an educational foundations or introduction to teaching course. No prior understanding of teaching is required, and the style is quite deliberately intended to draw the student into the material as quickly as possible. Using it early in the course can be beneficial, as the book addresses the desire many new teacher education students have to learn the "practical aspects" of teaching. The use of case studies helps to do that. At the same time, we try to show the need for conceptual and theoretical inquiry if one is to become an effective and reflective teacher. In the many years we have used the book, we have found it helpful as the first text in our teacher education courses.

If you have not taught or learned using the case method before, the following suggestions may be of some help. We also have learned through experience that it can be used to great advantage with in-service teachers who are still wrestling with their own hard-won conceptions of teaching.

1. It is important for the instructor and students to establish a good climate for discussion, one in which individuals feel free to express their views openly without fear of ridicule and also feel free to challenge the honest views of others with reasonable arguments and genuine alternatives.
2. Good group discussions are facilitated when all participants read cases and sketch their answers to case problems before class so a discussion can start with some forethought and direction.

3. Successful discussions epend upon the participants' careful listening to each other as much as it does on offering their ideas. It is also helpful to withhold quick appraisals of others' ideas until their point of view is genuinely understood and their reasons for taking their position heard.
4. Pedagogically, it is important for the instructor to summarize along the way, to help students see the ideas at issue, to bring in relevant theoretical knowledge, and to guide discussions to some reasonable conclusion, however firm or tentative.

This third edition adds another ending chapter reflecting on the three approaches and invites a broader consideration of our earlier treatments of them. We trust this will add richer dimension to the ongoing, thought-provoking discussions we expect users of this book to generate. For those who would like to react or comment on any aspect of this book, we invite e-mail sent to gfenster@umich.edu.

APPROACHES TO TEACHING

Chapter 1

Approaches to Teaching

This is a book about different approaches to teaching. In it we want to stimulate you to think about some basic ways to conceive of the role of the teacher. We believe that how you approach your teaching will have a great effect on what you do as a teacher. To help you see what we mean, we will begin with a sketch of the way three very different, yet quite effective teachers teach. You probably have had teachers like these yourself. Their ways of approaching teaching can be found in practice in any subject and on any level, even though here we have located them across a spectrum of grades and subjects. As you read about them, ask yourself: What makes them different? What do they take to be the main goal of teaching and the most important purpose of education? Do you find one more appealing than the others and a better fit with your own intuitions about good teaching?

Three Teachers

Jim Barnes has taught a number of different lower grades in the Bryant Elementary School over the past twelve years. The children like him. He is always firm and in command, but also kind and gentle. Jim believes that his contribution to the education of these youngsters is to give them both a set of basic skills that will be useful to them all their lives and a knowledge of specific subject matter that will allow them to successfully progress through their schooling and eventually become well-informed citizens in a democratic society.

He has experimented with a lot of different curriculum materials, but the ones he likes best and finds to be most effective share a number of common characteristics. They are highly organized and systematic, so the children can follow them easily. Because of their logical sequencing, the children are able to quickly develop useful patterns and strategies for dealing with them. They are progressive; that is, the children need what they learn today to be able to do the work tomorrow. Each new learning

1

builds on the last and leads to the next. Jim also relies on numerous nonthreatening evaluations so he can know exactly how each child is doing, what each needs help with, and when each is ready to move on. He prides himself on being a very efficient and effective teacher.

Most important, the children have a sense of accomplishment. They pride themselves on their achievements, and more than a few have stretched their parents' patience by insisting on reciting the whole of the multiplication tables or the Gettysburg Address, showing how they can solve ten difficult math problems, or classifying all living creatures in appropriate zoological categories. There is a spirit of "can-do" in Jim's classes. He leads and directs enthusiastically; he manages and executes skillfully; he judges and evaluates fairly. The materials make sense, and the work is doable. Jim is a successful teacher.

Nancy Kwong is also successful at what she does. She teaches English to middle school adolescents who are just beginning to discover who they are as persons. Nancy believes that the most important thing an education can give to youngsters is some perspective on themselves, on who and what they are, on who and what they might become. She teaches as if each word of literature they read was written for them to connect to their own life experiences. She finds that journal writing provides a real outlet for feelings and personal perspectives to grow and develop as well as a vehicle for encouraging a student's ability to communicate and write effectively.

Books are chosen by her students because they are about something *they* want to read about. There is no set curriculum. Any of the books in the school library are fair game. Class discussions are genuine dialogues, the sharing of reading experiences by equals. Nancy does not run the class as much as she runs with it. She shares her own perspectives and values with her students; they see her as a sympathetic, understanding, encouraging adult, unlike most of the other adults in their lives. They also see her as a teacher who cares about them as well as about the subject matter. There is no doubt about her love for literature and poetry. It shines in her eyes. There is no doubt in their minds either that she respects each one of them equally. It shows in her genuine interactions with each student. Nancy feels good about her nurturing relationship with young learners.

Roberto Umbras teaches history and social studies in an urban high school that is beset by the many problems of the inner city. For many, however, his classes are an island of calm in a sea of trouble. Racial and ethnic tension abound in his school. Roberto understands and respects cultural differences and tries to help his students do the same. He is, however, primarily a historian. His love for history began at an early age, and as he progressed through his studies, he came to the realization that the best way to learn history is to learn to be a historian. So that is how he approaches all his classes. Roberto believes that education should be an initiation into the many ways human beings have developed to make sense of their world. History and math, science and literature, music and art, all of the subjects are ways of knowing. The theories and methods of the social sciences, for example, are ways we have developed to understand the social world, and the skills and techniques of the historian help us unravel and make sense of our collective past.

His students quickly sense the difference in Roberto's classes. He treats them as people who can think, who can have valid opinions and ideas. They quickly learn, however, that ideas and opinions need to be backed up with facts. Historians cannot just tell interesting stories; they have to provide evidence for their claims and interpretations. Perhaps the most exciting thing they learn is that there is not just one true history. There are histories written from different national, cultural, and ethnic perspectives. There are different interpretations of the same historical event. History is written by human beings trying to make sense of the past, and no one is completely free of bias of some sort.

Roberto models the historian at work in many of his classes and asks his students to do the same. They collect primary materials and secondary sources dealing with an event or period of time. Conjectures and hypotheses are generated, and the materials are mined to see if sufficient data can be found to support their fledgling interpretations. Students really appreciate reading diaries and letters, other firsthand accounts and official reports. It makes history come alive for many for the first time. While few if any of them will ever become historians, they have, Roberto feels, an appreciation of the past, of differences in interpretation and cultural perspectives, and of a way to think and support claims made about human events. His students feel enabled.

How would you characterize the approaches of each of these teachers? Jim is trying to convey basic subject matter and skills as efficiently as possible. Nancy is trying to nurture the personhood of her students by engaging them in meaningful experiences that connect with their lives. Roberto is trying to get his students to think like historians and understand the way we try to make sense of the past. We could have exchanged these approaches across grade levels and subjects. For example, Jim's approach could be used in high school history. Nancy's approach could be used in Jim's elementary classes. And Roberto's approach could be used in middle school literature classes.

The important thing to realize here is that how teachers view their role and goals as teachers determines to a large extent how they will structure their teaching. In this book, we will help you explore and think about three very basic approaches to teaching. For convenience, we have named them the "executive," the "therapist," and the "liberationist" approaches, although they go by many names. Each has its historical roots as well as its contemporary research and scholarly support structure. But most important, each can give you a way to probe into your own intuitions about what you as a teacher should do.

You must remember, however, that these approaches are *conceptions* of teaching. They are ideas about what teaching is and should be. As such, they are products of the human mind and not some immutable reflection of the way the world really is. As such, they are also open to appraisal and criticism, adoption, rejection, or modification. They are three different perspectives that contemporary educators have used to conceive of the activities of teaching in ways that they think will help us do it better.

Three Approaches to Teaching

The executive approach views the teacher as an executor, a person charged with bringing about certain learnings, using the best skills and techniques available. Carefully developed curriculum materials and research on the effects of teaching are very important to this approach. They provide the teacher with techniques and understandings to use in the management of the classroom and the production of learning. Jim Barnes probably was using this approach.

The therapist approach views the teacher as an empathetic person charged with helping individuals grow personally and reach a high level of self-actualization, understanding, and acceptance. Psychotherapy, humanistic psychology, and existential philosophy underwrite this view, which focuses on students' developing their own selves as authentic persons through personally meaningful educational experiences. Nancy Kwong seems to have been using this approach.

The liberationist approach views the teacher as a liberator, a freer of the individual's mind and a developer of well-rounded, knowledgeable, rational, and moral human beings. Roberto Umbras may have been using it. The classical idea of a liberal education underwrites the contemporary mainstream version of this approach, and it is the one we will focus on in this book.[1]

We hope you can now see that there is much to learn and think about regarding approaches to teaching. Of course, one can teach without thinking about one's approach toward teaching just as one can be a lover or parent without giving much thought to the meaning of love or the duties and responsibilities of parenting. But we believe that professional teachers only become professionals when they reflect on and choose a stance toward their calling that guides and sustains them in their important work of educating persons. We also believe that, in this instance, knowledge is power. Knowing about different approaches to teaching will give you the power to choose ways to teach that will help you achieve the highest goals of one of the noblest of professions, helping individuals to become full-fledged persons. Moreover, understanding different approaches offers ways to think about what one is doing and what relation there is between what one intends as a teacher and what one actually does with learners. This is part of being a responsible, reflective, committed educator.

This may sound as if we will be asking you to choose one stance of the three we treat. As a matter of fact, we will be doing the opposite. We will be arguing that each approach contains within it values and purposes that are useful and appropriate in certain teaching situations, as well as being morally preferable in some instances. We may not convince you. In fact, we will display these approaches as basically incompatible and in conflict with each other. Therefore, you may see overriding reasons for adopting one stance over another. You would not be alone in that regard. You may argue for the consistency, correctness, or moral superiority of one position. All we will ask you to do regarding our position is to think seriously about the strengths and weaknesses of these approaches, about their appropriateness for dealing with human beings, and about your own commitments as an educator. However you end up, it will be *your* way and *your* view thoughtfully and deliberately chosen; and that is our goal as we encourage you to think about various approaches to teaching.

We end this book with a chapter of cases and disputes that we urge you to use selectively, as you go through each chapter, to focus and stimulate your thinking about important issues and applications of these basic approaches to teaching. For example, the case "Go Fly a Kite" at the end of chapter 6 provides an opportunity to see how three teachers of the same grade approach the same class project quite differently. You may want to turn to it now before going on.

Educating Persons

In our sketches of Jim Barnes, Nancy Kwong, and Roberto Umbras, we tried to help you see that what a teacher thinks teaching is—be it the efficient and effective management of learning, the therapeutic nurturing of personhood, or the freeing and developing of the mind by initiation into a way of knowing—determines the direction, tone, and style of the teacher. But something else also has a great influence on how teachers teach: their conception of what they would like their students eventually to become. What kinds of persons are good, happy, knowledgeable, productive persons, and how can education assist students in the process of becoming educated persons?

To help us try to answer this question, imagine that upon becoming an educated person individuals were issued an E-P card, a certificate about the size of a credit card. Across the top, in large, bold letters (just like the name of the bank on a credit card) is written **Educated Person**. What would entitle human beings to an E-P card? What would be its requirements? In order to be able to answer these questions (and perhaps to know if you can qualify for such a card yourself), you would need to be able to specify what an educated person is. That should not be too much of a problem. "An educated person is someone who has learned the basics: reading, writing, and arithmetic. . . . No, you need more than that. You need to graduate from high school. . . . No, college. . . . Wait a minute; some people graduate from high school and even from college without being very well educated. . . . Perhaps you also need to. . . . Oh, oh." Not quite so easy as it might at first seem! Let us start again.

You might say an educated person simply is anyone who graduates from some agreed upon institution of education, be it elementary school, high school, or college. That is all it takes to qualify. Then all would get E-P cards at graduation, just like everyone now gets diplomas. But we know some people with diplomas are not really educated and some who never got their diplomas have managed to educate themselves. So you might want to say that being an educated person requires more than just putting in time in an educational institution and graduating. You might think that an educated person should be one who has attained the acceptable level of knowledge and skill required for taking on the responsibilities of adulthood. But maybe even that is not enough. Perhaps being an educated person should also require knowledge of the classics, appreciation of art and music, and possession of a critical mind. Perhaps it should even require becoming a morally responsible human being. Or it might require even more than that. What do you think? What is your conception of an educated person?

Notice what is happening with these specifications. They begin at a very basic, no-nonsense level—an educated person is a graduate from some specified educational institution—and move all the way toward some grand conception of a full-fledged Educated Person. The definition shifts from being minimally descriptive to being increasingly prescriptive; from telling us what an educated person is in some ordinary sense, to telling us what one ought to be if one is to be considered a fully educated person in some ideal sense. As a definition like this one of "educated person" shifts in this way, philosophers say it is becoming more normative in character. *Normative* means evaluative, specifying desirable norms, characteristics, or standards. The idea of the normative is important, for it is almost impossible to talk about education and teaching without introducing normative value considerations. Educating is a normative activity directed at helping individuals develop into some image of what it means to be a full-fledged human being. More on this later as we discuss the different approaches and their different normative assumptions and implications. Let us get back to the E-P card.

One's eligibility for the card depends a great deal on the full meaning of "educated person." If an educated person is simply a graduate, then one only needs to attend school and achieve minimal standards to qualify for the card; everyone would get one at graduation. If, on the other hand, one needs to acquire certain characteristics to be fully recognized as an educated person, then some qualifying criteria must be met before obtaining the card. To understand what this means, let us simplify things and suppose that there were only four basic qualifying criteria in a certain society for eligibility to educated personhood. In that society, before an E-P card can be issued, a person must be able to (1) read and comprehend ordinary published materials (newspapers, books, maps, and nontechnical reports), (2) write and speak cogently, (3) make calculations needed in everyday life, and (4) be familiar with the laws and the constitution of the nation in which the individual lives.

If these four items were criteria for the card, you would know a lot more about a person who carried it than if merely being a graduate of some school was the sole criterion for the card. As a matter of fact, you might like these qualifying criteria so much that you think *everyone* minimally should meet them in the society in which you live, no matter what kind of school they attend or whether they graduate. After all, to be a good and productive citizen one should have to be verbally and mathematically literate, capable of being a self-sustaining, contributing member of society, and aware of the basic values, rights, and obligations of being a citizen.

In every society, some form of education is required of everyone to prepare them to play a constructive role in that society. When a society commits itself to the education of a majority of its children and youth, it typically establishes schools as places to carry out the task. In most nations of the world, such schools are government supported and attendance for children of certain ages is mandatory. In societies with large systems of publicly supported, mandatory schooling, it is often assumed that this is where children and youth go to earn their E-P cards.

Therefore, what a society determines an educated person to be—that is, what criteria it determines must be met before the E-P card is issued—also influences to a considerable degree what teachers do in their classrooms. If society says that the card is issued to those who can read, write, and calculate, that might influence the teacher's approach in one way. If society favors emotional well-being, mental health, and happiness over reading, writing, and calculation, then the teacher's approach is likely to be different. One's approach to teaching and one's conception of an educated person are tied together tightly.

A Helpful Formula

As we examine the several approaches to teaching in this book, it will be helpful to have a device to keep the significant features of each approach from being lost in the details of the discussion. We have already hinted at the complexity of the factors involved. In our own teaching about these approaches, we have found that a short formula will do the trick. It goes like this: $T\phi Sxy$. The symbol between the T and the S is the Greek letter *phi*. It designates an action. The formula is read as follows: The *teacher* (T) *teaches* (ϕ) the *student* (S) some *content* (x) in order to attain some *purpose* (y). This seemingly simple device carries enormous complexities, problems, issues, and insights in its wake.

Take, for example, the x or content part of the formula. Not only does the x designate certain subject areas, such as literature, mathematics, or history, it also symbolizes different aspects of the content to be acquired—as facts, as skills, as understandings, as beliefs, as sentiments, or even as traits of character. For example, suppose you are teaching chemistry and have the students do a distillation experiment. In addition to using this exercise to teach about states and phases (e.g., liquid, solid, gas), which is something (x_1) you want the students to *know about*, you also teach them (x_2) *how* to set up a distillation apparatus. Setting up the distillation apparatus is something you want the students to learn to be able *to do*; it is a skill, and as such is a kind of capability different from the knowledge they have about phases and states. Thus x can and often does have multiple meanings. It might designate any number of different kinds of student outcomes, and different approaches may stress different sets of these. For now, there is no need to get caught up in any of the complexities. Indeed, the point of the formula is to reduce the apparent complexity of the different approaches to teaching as we examine each one in depth. Here is another illustration of how the formula works.

Take the y symbol designating purpose in our formula. To what end (y) does the teacher engage the student in the study of some content (x)?

We will examine three major purposes in this book. The first is to acquire specified knowledge, the second is to become an authentic person, and the third is to liberate the mind. You will see how a change in y can alter ϕ and x dramatically. When the teacher undertakes teaching (ϕ) with the purpose of preparing the students to learn something in particular (y = executive purpose), then the teacher's approach to the student and to the content is very different from when the teacher sets out to free the mind of the student (y = liberationist purpose) or to develop the self (y = therapist purpose). For example, imagine a teacher of English literature using the executive approach. He or she probably would structure the course and individual lessons in ways designed to prepare students to go on to take more advanced courses in English literature and perhaps eventually to become specialists in English literature. Emphasis would be on covering the field and gaining specific knowledge.

Imagine another teacher using the liberationist approach. He or she might teach students English literature with the primary intention of getting them to think about aspects of human nature and human emotions not likely to be encountered in their everyday experiences and helping them to see and understand other ways of thinking about and perceiving the world. This teacher believes that, just as travel broadens the mind, so does learning about things beyond one's immediate ken. It frees one from the narrowness of one's own small world.

Imagine a third teacher using the therapist approach. He or she might use literature to help students see into their own souls, to help them recognize their own feelings and values in ways they might not have been able to articulate before. Becoming educated for this teacher is coming to know and forming one's self authentically. Teaching is helping people become their real selves.

Which literature teacher would you rather have? Do you already have a predisposition toward one of these approaches? Before going on to the next chapter, in which we will more fully examine the executive approach, you may want to look in chapter 6 at the case "Grading Policies" and at the dispute over what it really means to be "An Educated Person." This will give you a chance to examine your own predispositions toward these approaches and the concept of Educated Person before you begin a more rigorous study of these important issues. There is also a case in chapter 6 called "School and Approach Mismatch" that raises another problem with choosing your own approach. You will see that there is much to think about in this regard.

Chapter 2

The Executive Approach

Classrooms are complex places. Often twenty-five to thirty-five children are contained in a rather tight space, along with one or two adults. There is a great deal going on. The children are there because they are supposed to be there, and the teachers are trying to engage their students in the study of whatever content is prescribed. The complexity of classrooms, when joined with the demand that certain things take place there, means that they must in some way be managed.

Managing a Classroom

How do you manage a classroom? Think about it. Your task is to engage the students in academic work of some sort. To do that, you have to determine what they are to be taught (curriculum guides might help here). Then you must figure out whether the students who are in *your* classroom are able (ready) to learn what is prescribed for them. After you have diagnosed the students to determine their readiness for the material you want to present, you may find that they are not quite up to it. You may have to revise the material, adapting it to make it accessible to your students. Once you have the material ready, you have to figure out how to get it across. What motivational devices might be used to interest the students and keep them engaged? What classroom structure best contributes to successful learning—small groups, large groups, whole-class instruction, or independent learning?

And this is only the *planning* stage. After you figure out what is to be done, then you must do it. No matter how well you plan, events will occur that cause you to veer from your plan. In the course of teaching, you are constantly making decisions about the students, the material, and the overall success or failure of your efforts. You probably will revise your plan many times while on your feet teaching the lesson.

Then after you teach it, you may follow up with an evaluation, only to find that a mere six out of twenty-eight students understood more than half of what you taught. Now you have to reteach the unit, but you are stymied about how to reconstruct it so that most of the students will understand it.

All this complexity requires careful planning, action carried out on the basis of the plan (although with many revisions en route), then follow-up evaluation, revised plans, and another instructional effort. These are the kinds of things that executives do. They plan, execute the plan, appraise their effort, then revise and act again. Executives, by and large, manage people and resources. They make decisions about what people will do, when they will do it, how long it is likely to take, and what standard of performance determines whether to move on to the next task or repeat the old one.

Until recently very little thought was given to the teacher as an executive. On the contrary, teachers were thought simply to be experts in the subjects they taught, while students were willing participants in the teaching of these subjects. The task of teaching seemed fairly straightforward: Just get the youngsters together, present them with a well-constructed lesson, and you could go home knowing that you did a day's work well. This view prevailed for a good part of the last century and most of this one. Then researchers began studying actual classroom settings. They found them far more complex than the folk wisdom of the time had led most people to believe. And they found teachers engaged in more complex and sophisticated endeavors than they had traditionally been given credit for.

As our understanding of the complexity of the classroom situation emerged from research on teaching, it became clear that teachers were more than subject-matter experts with interesting gimmicks for getting that subject matter across to their students. What the researchers found were teachers who managed classroom aides, dealt with angry parents, handled school administrators who sometimes intervened in classrooms in unhelpful ways, coped with irrelevant or inappropriate textbooks and supplementary materials, and spent great amounts of time complying with policy mandates from local, state, and federal regulations; all this, *plus* teaching the students in their classes.

Not surprisingly, researchers were impressed that teachers faced all these tasks and pressures and handled them with varying degrees of success. Some researchers (particularly David Berliner[1]) found the metaphor of the executive to be an accurate and helpful one to use in understanding the work of a teacher. However, it was not simply the pressure and complexity of the classroom that made the executive metaphor appealing. Something else emerged from the early studies of teachers. It seemed that effective teaching might be analyzed into a discrete set of generic, or common, skills. That is, regardless of the grade level, the nature of the students, the subject matter, or the culture of the school, certain instructional practices seemed to be regularly associated with gains in student achievement, while other instructional practices appeared unrelated to student mastery of content. Discrete executive skills for teaching could be identified.

For example, the practice of acting friendly with the class—discussing ballgames, the national news, or the gossip around school—is *not* a practice associated with gains in student learning. Indeed, the avoidance of academic work in classrooms has been the subject of several fascinating studies, wherein researchers have noted that teachers and students forge "treaties" or "bargains" to sidestep rigorous academic work in favor of relaxed and pleasant relationships in the classroom.[2] Although the concept of student–teacher treaties was not developed when the studies on instructional time began, the absence of academic work was evident enough to alert Berliner and other researchers to the importance of the time variable in student learning.[3] They rediscovered a very simple idea: By and large, students learn what they study, and how much they learn is in large measure determined by how much time they are engaged in that study.

Not surprising, is it? What is surprising is the way teachers dealt with time. Consider a distinction that comes from one of the most famous of the instructional time studies, the Beginning Teacher Evaluation Study (BTES).[4] BTES researchers distinguished between allocated time and engaged time. Allocated time is how much time a teacher or school sets aside for the study of some subject. Engaged time is the time a *given student* actually works at the subject. What the researchers found is that elementary schools and teachers varied widely in allocated time for the different subjects. Some teachers would, for example, allocate forty-five minutes a day to math, while others would allocate thirty minutes; some would allocate thirty-five minutes to science, others would hardly touch science study; some teachers always devoted forty to fifty minutes a day to social studies, while others would allocate zero to fifteen minutes to it some days and sixty to ninety minutes on other days.

Time on Task

Clearly the amount of time allocated to a subject makes a tremendous difference in students' opportunity to learn it. If the teacher does not spend much time with math, then it is not surprising that his or her students fare poorly on math exams. However, this variation in allocated time was not the big surprise of the research on instructional time. The big surprise was in engaged time. By focusing on selected students in a classroom, the researchers clocked the amount of time these target students were engaged in the assigned activity, or "on-task." What they found was that, even though a teacher might *allocate* fifty minutes to math, a student might be on-task only seven or eight of those fifty minutes! The engaged time for the student was less than 20 percent of the allocated time.

Consider the impact of this finding. If, in general, students learn subject content only if they study it (you do not learn what you do not study), and the amount of that learning is directly related to the amount of time spent studying (the more you study the more you learn, generally speaking), then in order to learn something well it is necessary to spend a fair amount of time with it. However, by looking at selected students, it was found that some students spent only seven out of fifty minutes on the actual academic task. How could this happen? It is far easier to slip up than you might think. Consider this example.

You set aside fifty minutes for the math unit. It begins right after recess, which ends at 10:35 A.M. The students do not get back at the same time, so you wait until they are all in their seats. Time: 10:39. There are some announcements and a few things you want them to know about activities this afternoon and later this week. Time: 10:41. There is an outburst in the back of the room. You settle that. Time: 10:42. You start the math lesson with some directions about a task you want everybody to do in his or her workbook, saying that they should take ten minutes for this assignment and then the whole class will discuss it. You spend some time explaining how you want students to do the task. These instructions are not teaching them anything about math, only about how to complete the workbook pages. Time: 10:46. Eleven minutes gone and no math activity has occurred yet.

At last the students are working in the books. It so happens that Harry, however, did not really understand your instructions. Because he is rather shy, he does not raise his hand for help. It is 10:49 before you notice him doodling on the margin of the book. You walk back to his desk and clear up the confusion; he begins to work fifteen minutes after the scheduled beginning of the math period. Within two minutes, he is confused. He puzzles over the difficulty for a while, then stops working. It is 10:53 and Harry is off-task again. You are busy with the other students, so do not notice his problem. He is too embarrassed to ask for help, especially since you were somewhat exasperated with him the time before. He waits until you start class discussion to learn the solution to the problem that threw him off. You are a little late getting the group started in discussion. It is 10:58 before the discussion begins.

Harry goes back on-task at the beginning of the discussion and stays with you for the duration of the discussion, which concludes at 11:11. Thus he was on-task for thirteen minutes of the discussion plus two minutes during the workbook exercise. Thirty-six minutes of allocated time have elapsed, and Harry has accumulated fifteen minutes of engaged time. You have a chance to increase the percentage of Harry's engaged time by managing the remaining fourteen minutes of allocated time so that Harry can be actively involved in the content of the lesson. But that does not happen because you look at the clock, note that it is 11:11 and that the period is scheduled to end at 11:25, and conclude that it is not worthwhile for you to begin another unit with so little time remaining. So you assign the students to their workbooks in order to fill the remaining time. Harry goes along just fine for three more minutes, then becomes stumped again. You are not monitoring student seatwork, however, so you do not see him gazing out the window. You have an attendance report due by 11:30, so you take these few minutes to complete it. At 11:25 you call the math period to a halt. Harry has been on-task in the study of math for only eighteen of the fifty minutes, just about 35 percent of the available time. Not good, but how much engaged time do you think the other students in your class had?

Features of This Approach

Researchers have found that there are many ways for teachers to increase the time that students are engaged. These skills for managing learning time are considered generic teaching skills because they appear to be unrelated to student background characteristics like race or home environment, to the subject matter taught, or to the nature of the school setting. The teacher is seen as manager of classroom time, as one who makes decisions about the way student time will be used in the classroom. Time engaged in academic work is not, however, the only aspect of the executive approach to teaching. Three other elements have been identified as having a major impact on the effectiveness of a teacher's efforts.[5] They are cues, corrective feedback, and reinforcement. Cues are like maps and signposts; the teacher employs them to alert students to what is to be learned and how to go about learning it. Teachers who make extensive use of cues, particularly in the early segments of an instructional sequence, often have a stronger impact on learning than those who do not use cues. The same can be said for corrective feedback, wherein teachers quickly remedy errors in written and oral work. Reinforcement, ranging from a fleeting smile through marks on report cards all the way to such tangible rewards as food, toys, or money, is also quite powerful as an instructional technique, although it requires experience and insight into the learner to employ it well.

Another aspect of the executive approach is known as opportunity to learn—giving students the chance to learn what is being taught. Sometimes teachers embark on complex topics or ideas but allow too little opportunity for students to become involved in these topics to the extent that the topics demand. The material is covered too quickly, without adequate background preparation, or is misrepresented in order to cover it in the short time allowed. Any of these factors denies the student adequate opportunity to learn the material.

There is an interesting facet to all these features of the executive approach to teaching. They all place a high premium on student learning. What is so strange about that? Is not student learning what schools and teachers are all about? Well, yes . . . in a way. The difficulty arises when we ask what the students are learning and how that learning is assessed. Let us look at the assessment issue for a moment. The formula $(T\phi Sxy)$ discussed in the last chapter will help here.

Recall that the x stands for the content to be learned. The teacher strongly disposed toward the executive approach views x as specific facts, ideas, topics, or perspectives to be gotten into the heads of the learners. The executive skills we looked at above are the means for moving this specified knowledge from its classroom source (text, supplementary material, lectures, and so forth) to its destination (the student's mind). Remember that ϕ in $T\phi Sxy$? It is the activity of teaching. In this case, ϕ is teaching that is characterized by extensive use of executive skills, including time-management techniques, matching content taught to what the tests measure, and establishing sufficient opportunity to learn.

The purpose (y) of this activity is that students will acquire the specific knowledge communicated by the teacher. Thus, in the executive approach to teaching, $T\phi Sxy$ can be interpreted as follows: The teacher (T) uses certain organizational and management skills (ϕ) to impart to students (S) specific facts, concepts, skills, and ideas (x) so that these students are most likely to acquire and retain this specified knowledge (y). This conception of teaching emphasizes direct connections between what the teacher does and what the student learns. Indeed, the form of research used to study many of the practices that make up the executive approach to teaching is called "process-product research." The process is the teacher's activity (ϕ), while the product is the student's mastery of what is taught (y). The literature about this form of teaching is often called "teacher-effectiveness" literature, because so much stress is placed on the effectiveness of the classroom teacher.

Criticisms

If you pursue the assumptions and implications of the executive approach to teaching, certain disturbing things turn up. The teacher seems like the manager of a kind of production line, where students enter the factory as raw material and are somehow "assembled" as persons (they earn their Educated-Person card by successfully acquiring the specified knowledge dispensed at school). The teacher is not so much an actual part of the process as a manager of it. The teacher is not, it seems, "inside" the process of teaching and learning but "outside," where he or she regulates the content and the activities of the learner. Indeed, some critics have viewed the time-management aspects of the executive approach as akin to an oarmaster on an ancient slave ship—the one who stands, beating a large drum, to keep the rowers on-task.

These characterizations of the executive approach—as factory manager, production-line supervisor, or slave-ship oarmaster—offend our sensibilities about education. Most of us do not like to think about children, learning, school, and teaching along the same lines as factories or slave ships. Yet the executive approach invites comparison to such things. It stresses attention to task, performance of duty, achievement results, and accountability for failure to produce. The executive approach seems to disregard parts of education that many think are of utmost importance, such as the nature and interests of individual students, the special characteristics of different subject matters, and the varying demands that differences in geography, economics, and culture make on what takes place in school.

What do you think? Are you ready to abandon this approach as unfaithful to your ideals of education? Are you disappointed that what seemed a useful way to approach teaching turns out to have such unsavory features? Or will you hold on to this approach in the belief that its value outweighs its faults? What are the arguments for holding on to it? Let us take a look.

In the introductory chapter you met Jim Barnes, the elementary school teacher who prided himself on his ability to teach specific subject matter. Imagine that you are Jim. You want your fifth-grade students to master computing the area of plane surfaces bounded by straight lines —that is, to learn the formula $(A = bh)$ and to be able to apply it correctly. You have a clear idea of the x you want to get across. What about the ϕ? How are you going to teach all those Ss this x? Why not use the executive approach? It seems ideally suited to this outcome. In fact, it appears as if you would be a fool not to approach this teaching task according to the executive approach. Bring the class together right away, discuss the objective of this lesson, teach the lesson clearly and without exceeding the students' ability to comprehend you, assign seatwork so that students can practice what you are teaching them, monitor their seatwork closely, follow up with a clarification presentation, check for understanding, then test to determine whether they mastered the content. Could there be any better way?

Maybe. Think about some things that are missing from this little scenario. Do the students have any interest in computing the surface area? Are they able to perceive a value or use for this knowledge? Is there a better way to introduce this material? Will what they learn from Jim enhance their understanding of mathematics? Will any of them ever wonder how to compute areas bounded by curved lines? Does Jim care very much about his lesson (do you?), or is he teaching it because this is what is next in the textbook that the school district has adopted? If you want some answers to these questions, do not look to the executive approach. This approach deals primarily with generic skills of teaching, skills that are independent of the content taught, the context in which teaching occurs, and the backgrounds of the students and teachers.

Teacher Effectiveness

If the executive approach does not account for content, context, or culture, what is its value? We have already looked at one answer to this question. Its value is that it provides a very clear, straightforward means to move some specified knowledge from a source (for example, a book, teacher, or film) to the mind of the learner. Indeed, if followed with care, the executive approach increases the probability that more of the students will learn more of the content than would otherwise be the case. As one prominent researcher put it, "teacher effectiveness refers to the ability of a classroom teacher to produce higher than predicted gains on standardized achievement tests."[6] Why is it important that x be moved from source to student as efficiently and effectively as possible? Just a bit of recent history answers this question and throws a great deal of light on the executive approach to teaching.

The school-as-factory analogy has been around for a long time in American education, and so has the doctrine that schools ought to be efficient. Both these ideas emerged late in the last century. But the notion that an effective teacher is one who produces higher-than-predicted gains in student achievement (as measured by standardized tests) is an idea barely past the age of majority. It got its start in the stimulus-response-reward psychology of Edward L. Thorndike in the early twentieth century and gained legitimacy by midcentury in the work on operant conditioning by the famous behavioral psychologist B. F.

Skinner. In 1954, in a paper suggestively entitled "The Science of Learning and the Art of Teaching," Skinner contended that "the whole process of becoming competent in any field must be divided into a very large number of very small steps, and reinforcement [i.e., reward] must be contingent upon the accomplishment of each step."[7] Ten years later he stated the point even more boldly: "The application of operant conditioning to education is simple and direct. Teaching is the arrangement of contingencies of reinforcement under which students learn."[8] In simple terms, teachers could bring about the learning they sought from students by knowing precisely when and how to reward students for behaviors that increasingly approximated the goals set for them.

Skinner's contentions about teaching and learning set the stage for two things. First, they encouraged many educators to strip away much of the mystique about teaching as an ineffable human activity. Second, they led educational researchers to draw a tighter loop around the interaction between teacher and learner. The notion of teaching as stimulus, or cause, and learning as response, or effect, enabled researchers to focus exclusively on these two behaviors, without becoming sidetracked by the family backgrounds of students, their life histories, or the particular subject matter to be learned. Skinner's work had a powerful effect on the conceptions that many of us have about teaching and learning, and how the former affects the latter.

These conceptions might not have influenced the actual practice of education too extensively, save for some events taking place in the political and economic sectors of our society at the time. Following the *Brown v. Board of Education* decision in 1954, the federal government made ever-increasing commitments to schooling as an instrument for the eradication of poverty and ignorance among racial and ethnic minorities. These commitments reached a very high intensity in the mid-sixties with President Lyndon Johnson's Great Society programs, such as Head Start, Follow Through, and Parent-Child Centers. As more and more dollars were channeled into education, policy makers became increasingly curious about how the money was being spent and whether it was actually helping the students for whom it was targeted.

The Coleman Report

As part of the Civil Rights Act of 1964, Congress mandated a study of equal educational opportunity among various racial and ethnic groups. This study was directed by James Coleman and is most frequently referred to as the Coleman Report.[9] Its purpose was to examine the relationship between various factors and educational achievements. Using a massive sample of 600,000 students, 60,000 teachers, and 4,000 schools, Coleman found that the amount of money spent on schools did not seem to make much difference in the achievement of those who attended them. He found that different racial groups attended different schools, that the physical differences among these schools were not all that great, that such differences in facilities and professional personnel as he could find did not make much difference in what students accomplished, and that white students often learned far more in their schools than students belonging to other racial and ethnic groups learned in theirs.

That last sentence says a great deal. You might want to read it again. According to Coleman, equality of educational achievement was not obtained by making educational facilities equal. What made an educational difference was the background of the students (particularly parents' income and educational levels). Coleman's data indicated that student peers had a far stronger influence on educational attainment (or lack of it) than the quality of the school's physical facilities, the richness of its curriculum, or the preparation of its teachers. These findings were devastating for educators, who thought that they and their schools had a dramatic impact on student learning.

To understand exactly what is going on here, we have to look at the notion of variance in student achievement. We know, for example, that in 1964 blacks and whites, as groups, varied dramatically in what they learned in school. Once you accept that fact, then the question centers on what accounts for this large variation in achievement. Coleman argued that family background and peer influence accounted for most of the variance and that schools and teachers had little effect on the variance. That was the conclusion that bothered educators, cast doubt on Great Society programs, and led those who controlled educational dollars to look harder at how they were being spent.

After the initial shock of the Coleman Report, researchers began to find flaws in it. The first questions were about the statistics used to analyze the data, then about the design of the study, and, inevitably, about the validity of the conclusions. New research programs were begun, programs that were particularly pointed at finding out whether Coleman was correct.

Research on Teaching

The behaviorists' cause-and-effect conception of teaching and learning shaped most of the educational research programs for two decades following the Coleman study. Researchers viewed teaching as a discrete set of behaviors and tried to find whether different sets of behaviors were related to different learning gains by students. These researchers assumed a tight connection between teaching as a cause and learning as an effect that follows from the cause. The researchers were not burdened with fancy ideas about the nobility of teaching, nor did they pay much attention to the so-called inputs of education (such as the size of the school library, per-pupil expenditure, or the number of college recruiters who visited the school in a year). On the contrary, they went straight for the jugular. They had one burning question: Do the instructional behaviors of some teachers lead to systematic gains in student achievement, while different instructional behaviors by other teachers show no systematic gains in student learning?

It is because of the work of the behaviorists and other experimental psychologists that researchers possessed confidence in this way of phrasing the key questions. In addition, recent advances in research design and data analysis permitted researchers to look directly into classrooms for an answer. Moreover, the federal government, through the newly established National Institute of Education (now known as the Office of Educational Research and Improvement), was anxious to fund this research. If the researchers could show that what goes on in schools does account for some of the variance in student achievement, the government's past investment in education would be vindicated and future investment continued.

At first the research programs yielded little. But gradually findings began to emerge showing that teachers do make a difference (one of the key books at the time was entitled *Teachers Make a Difference*[10]) and that what happens in schools does account for some of the variance in student achievement. Despite continuing progress in this form of research, however, no one, to the best of our knowledge, has succeeded in showing that what teachers and schools do ever accounts for more than 15 percent, or at most 20 percent, of the variance in achievement. Still, that is no mean feat. Time in school does not consume more than 20 percent of the waking life of the student, so perhaps it would be unreasonable to expect that what happens there would account for any more of the variance.

The teaching behaviors found to be associated with optimum gains in student learning are those that we have already discussed as the executive approach to teaching. Now it should be clear why this approach is independent of content, context, and culture. The researchers set out to find the generic links between teaching and learning, using conceptions of teaching and learning gained from the work of behavioral and experimental psychologists. They framed their studies to address the perplexing problems revealed by the Coleman Report and a government committed to achieving equality of educational opportunity. What they learned is that there are some instructional behaviors that are more frequently associated with high gains in student achievement than other instructional behaviors.

Beginning in the late 1970s and continuing through the last decade, research on teaching has shifted away from the process-product models to studies that incorporate a far more extensive array of research methods and designs, as well as more complex conceptions of teaching, learning, and classrooms. Indeed some of the more recent research examines all three of these elements at once, focusing on the interactions among teachers, students, and subject matter within the specific setting of the school classroom. The work of Walter Doyle is among the best known of this genre of research.

Doyle is concerned with the way teachers and students interact to define the nature of the work that students do. He contends that while "teachers affect what students learn by describing specifications for assignments, providing explanations about the processes that can be used to accomplish work, serving as a resource while students are working, and managing accountability for products," the essential element of teaching is "the way teachers define and structure the work students are to do."[11] Doyle looks at the curriculum in classrooms as a "bundle of tasks," which teachers both structure and enact. In so doing, the teacher converts the official curriculum into a series of concrete events. The challenge for the teacher is to convert or translate curriculum in ways that generate tasks that are educative for the students. Given that so many tasks are designed to simply occupy students' time or manage their conduct in workgroups, the design and enactment of educative tasks is not a simple undertaking for the teacher.

Although different from the studies of instructional time, and definitely outside the category of process-product research, Doyle's work may still be thought of as contributing to the executive approach to teaching. As in the case of the instructional time studies, the study of academic task structures advances our understanding of how teachers and students engage in classroom events and activities that are either educative or noneducative. Doyle, like Berliner, is interested in assisting teachers in becoming more effective and productive. Doyle's work, however, rests on the view that what happens in classrooms is more a matter of the interactive dynamic among students, teachers, and subject matter, and less a matter of the teacher's simply assuming authority for directing and controlling events in the classroom.

Afterthoughts

This approach to teaching can be viewed as a very powerful one. No other set of instructional methods can lay claim to accounting for so much (relatively speaking) of the variance in student achievement. But consider this: Suppose we took teaching out of the typical school classroom and placed it in a tutorial setting. Suppose there are only two or three students to one teacher. And suppose further that these few students know why they are studying with this teacher and willingly choose to be part of an educational relationship. Do you think the executive approach to teaching would be of much value in this setting? It would seem that knowledge and skill about engaged time, curriculum matched with evaluation, opportunity to learn, and all the other aspects of the executive approach are superfluous in this new setting.

Why? Because there is hardly anything that needs organizing or managing. The teacher is free to concentrate specifically on the students and on what they are learning. What does this perspective tell you about the executive approach? Take a moment to think about it. Let us see if your answer is the same as ours.

If the executive approach is unnecessary in a tutorial setting, yet seemingly necessary in a typical school classroom, then this approach to teaching may have much more to do with how we organize education in schools and how we engage learners in this form of education than it does with any root notion of what education is all about. To put it another way, the executive approach to teaching accounts for variance in achievement, not because it has been shown to be a particularly good way to educate human beings, but because it works well in rooms of 600 square feet that are filled with twenty-five young people, more than two-thirds of whom, if given a choice, are likely to choose to be somewhere else.

The executive approach to teaching seems to work because it fits so well the modern circumstances of teaching. If we changed the circumstances, the executive approach might be far less powerful. The power of the approach stems from its connection to the structure of modern-day schooling: to classrooms with a lot of students; to accountability; to tests and report cards; to grade levels and diplomas; to teachers who are licensed to work with some children but not others, with some subjects but not others.

Still, these are the realities of the schools in which we work and learn. Are we compelled to adopt an approach to teaching that capitalizes nicely on the structural and organizational features of schooling, while leaving untouched many of the truly basic values that constitute our sense of what it means to be an educated person? Or are Fenstermacher and Soltis merely engaging in sophistry here, inasmuch as there is no inherent conflict in both managing a classroom as any good executive would manage a complex organization and, at the same time, pursuing and attaining the ideals of a fully educated human being? We hope you are stymied by this problem. It has been a difficult one for us to handle ourselves. The resolution might lie in looking at another approach to teaching. Before you begin the next chapter, however, we urge you to examine the relevant cases and disputes in chapter 6. If you take a few moments to work through those that bear on the executive approach, as indicated in table 1, you will not only have a better idea of this approach but also be better prepared to venture into an examination of the next approach to teaching.

Chapter 3

The Therapist Approach

Remember Nancy Kwong, the English teacher? She let her students choose the books they wanted to read. She also had them keep a journal so they could reflect on how they felt about what they read and who they were becoming. What does how you feel about something have to do with teaching and learning? A great deal, especially in the therapist approach to teaching. But we have to be careful here. It is easy to trivialize this approach, reducing it to some formless amalgam of emotions, beliefs, attitudes, and opinions. Care is also required to avoid concluding that this approach has something to do with persons who are not mentally healthy. Though it might be a useful approach for those whose grasp of reality is less well developed, the therapist approach is intended to apply as much to the everyday activities of teaching as the executive and liberationist approaches. Just why this approach is called the therapist approach will become clear as the chapter unfolds. As we did with the executive approach, let us begin by considering what might be an actual situation.

You are hired to teach English to intermediate school children (say, grade 8). Some weeks before school begins, you start seriously preparing for the first weeks of school. What thoughts run through your head as you sit with paper, textbooks, and other class materials in front of you? Are you thinking about how you will approach the grammar lessons? The assigned textbook appears to do a good job of explaining key grammatical ideas, although you might want to expand some sections and shorten others.

How about literature? How will you balance linguistic and literary considerations over the course of the year? As you ponder these questions, you are probably thinking about the students—wondering about the best way to elicit their interest in what you plan to teach. But who are these students you have in mind? Do they have names? Do you know anything about them? What do they care about, and what is their interest, if any, in the study of English?

Individual Differences

Often when new teachers plan their instruction, they have in mind some prototypical student: someone like themselves, perhaps, or an archetype they recall from their own days as students. This conception of the prototypical student usually shapes the way a new teacher plans to teach the subject. Let us say this happens to you. You do all your preliminary planning with prototypical students in mind. It is not only convenient for you to do it this way, it may also be necessary; how can anybody really plan for students they have not seen? For that matter, how can anybody *really* take account of the lives of students? They differ in so many fundamental ways.

Just to show you how pertinent these doubts are, here is a sneak preview of your eighth-grade English class—the one you will not see for four more weeks. The characteristics or conditions of the learners are indicated, and the number of students who share each condition is shown.

Characteristic	Number of Students
English is not native language; speaks only native language	4
English is not native language; speaks English adequately	4
Physical handicap: missing thumb and two fingers on right hand	1
Moderate hearing impairment	2
Parents separated within the year	1
Parents divorced	6
First year in this school district; moved from more than a hundred miles away	5
Has extreme difficulty with spatial representation; possible neural damage	1
Detests English grammar	5
Loves English grammar	2
Shows no apparent feeling toward English grammar	13
Reads well above grade level	7
Reads at grade level	6
Reads well below grade level	11
Five merit badges short of Eagle scout	1
Physically abused by one or both parents	2
Traveled to more than five foreign countries	2
Traveled to more than five U.S. states	15
Never traveled beyond twenty-five miles of home	7

Has recurring nightmares; gets little sleep	1
Loves nearly all sports and rock stars	5
Is very selective about rock stars and sports	12
Enjoys building things	6
Responds well to freedom and responsibility	8
Responds well to structure and authority	8
Family survives primarily on welfare	3
Family consists of two adults and two children; no fewer than two cars and home larger than 10 rooms	3

As you read through this list of characteristics of your future students, did you think of a way to deal with them pedagogically? Or did you find yourself wishing they would just go away?

You, as the teacher, have some choices here. You can ignore these conditions, trying to teach past them and hoping for the best. That may sound like a terrible thing to do, but a lot of teachers feel they must do so, at least part of the time. With twenty to thirty-five students in a class, a required amount of content to be covered, tests to be taken, and grades to be given, some teachers argue that they are simply unable to deal with the multiple characteristics of their students. Though these teachers have a point, there are alternatives to this position.

Another way to approach the individual differences among students is to acknowledge them, but more as impediments or facilitators to learning than as vital parts of the learning process itself. This point may seem like a distinction without a difference, but it is crucial to understanding the therapist approach to teaching. The teacher who treats student characteristics as impediments or facilitators to learning is placing a high value on the student's acquiring the content of instruction. There is a content, some x, out there, so to speak, that the teacher is trying to convey to the learner. The particular characteristics of the learner impede or expedite this process of imparting x to S, and the teacher tries to take these characteristics into account so that they support, rather than hinder, the acquisition of x. The individual differences of the student count only insofar as the teacher can use or surmount them to bring about the learning of some specified subject matter.

Features of This Approach

So far we have looked at two alternatives to dealing with student characteristics. You might ignore them, which, given the typical circumstances of today's classroom, is not always so heinous a deed as it may seem at first. Or you might acknowledge these characteristics in ways that diminish those likely to hinder learning and enhance those likely to facilitate learning. There is a third alternative. You might treat these characteristics as essential features of the learning process itself, as vital to everything the learner thinks, feels, and does. In this view, what the learner *is* cannot be separated from what is learned and how it is learned.

That handy little formula, $T\phi Sxy$, will help us amplify this point. In the executive approach, x symbolizes subject-matter content: geology, perhaps, or physics, history, or auto mechanics. The ϕ stands for the technical skills used to get x from its source to the learner, in a way that permits the learner to acquire x to some acceptable level of competence. The point of the activity (y) is the learner's acquisition of specialized knowledge. In the therapist approach to teaching, the character of ϕ is altered: Teaching is the activity of guiding and assisting the learner (S) to select and pursue x. The act of teaching (ϕ) is much less involved in preparing content (x) for S to acquire and is far more involved in preparing S for the tasks of choosing, working on, and evaluating what is learned.

The purpose of teaching in the therapist approach is to enable the learner to become an authentic human being, a person capable of accepting responsibility for what he or she is and is becoming, a person able to make choices that define one's character as one wishes it to be defined. To the teacher as therapist, the student's authenticity is not cultivated by acquiring remote knowledge that is unrelated to the quest for personal meaning and identity. Filling the student's head with specified knowledge that has been selected, packaged, and conveyed by others only keeps the student from grasping himself as a human being. It separates the student from himself by forcing him to attend, not to his own feelings, thoughts, and ideas, but to the sterile thoughts, images, and attitudes of others.

The teacher as therapist, dealing with the student characteristics described in the long list above, would neither ignore these characteristics nor try to use them as mechanisms to support the learning of some bookish content. The teacher as therapist would confront these characteristics directly, often openly with the affected student, and ask how the student plans to develop herself and experience her world, given her particular characteristics. The teacher as therapist does not accept responsibility for moving specific knowledge and skills from some outside source into the mind of the learner; rather the teacher accepts responsibility for helping the student make the choice to acquire knowledge of a given kind and for supporting the student as she acquires that knowledge and uses it to advance her sense of self.

How does one get an Educated-Person card according to the therapist approach to teaching? Answering this question requires breaking the rules a bit. The idea of such a card would be anathema to the teacher as therapist, for reasons that will become clear when we examine the existential foundation for the therapist approach. For now, we will bend the rules a bit. The card comes when the person is an authentic human being. To be authentic is to be genuine (not false or deceptive, especially to yourself), to take your freedom seriously, to understand that you have choices about who and what you are, and to accept the responsibility for making these choices and confronting their consequences.

The y in the therapist version of $T\phi Sxy$ is authenticity. That is the purpose of undertaking a relationship between teacher and learner. When that y is achieved, the E-P card is earned. In the executive approach, the y is specialized knowledge. Teacher and learner come together for the purpose of the learner's acquiring specific knowledge and skills. When the specialized knowledge and skills are mastered to some agreed level of competence (often determined by scores on tests), the E-P card is awarded to the learner. The x for the executive teacher is content selected by the teacher or curriculum specialist. In contrast, the therapist teacher is committed to assisting S to learn the x of his choice. There is a definite difference. In the executive approach, $T\phi Sxy$ reads "the Teacher teaches (ϕ) x to S so that y (S acquires specialized knowledge)." In the therapist approach, $T\phi Sxy$ reads "the T guides and assists (ϕ) S in the selection and learning of x so that y (S becomes an authentic, self-actualized person)." Note that the object of the verb changes from the executive to the therapist approach; it is content in the former case, an attribute of the student himself in the latter case.

Consider the following description of her classes by a therapist teacher of writing. It should help you to see the contrast between the therapist and executive approaches more clearly.

I teach writing to two very different groups of students, but I teach it in essentially the same way to both groups. The first group might be described as a heterogeneously representative sample of sixth graders from our affluent suburb. The students in the Alternative High School program, on the other hand, are harder to describe. These students have for all intents and purposes "quit" school. They have stopped attending class on a regular basis, and probably, have not paid attention in class for many years. Their lives are rich in turmoil and trouble. Their parents can in almost every case be best described as dysfunctional, by which I mean that something has gone terribly awry in their parenting. The students physically abuse each other and their peers, and suffer abuse at the hands of others as a matter of course. Many are in trouble with the law, or have been at one time or another. They suffer an intense lack of self-esteem. When I began teaching them, it became clear to me that they could not succeed in an academic setting unless this lack of self-esteem was addressed in some way. I have tackled this primarily through writing.

I tell all my students that writing is important because it comes directly from inside of them. I believe that writing comes from a union of the mind and soul, and that it is the most personal thing students are asked to do in school. Consequently, when I ask students to write, I feel a strong obligation to be supportive of them and to encourage and praise them for their efforts as unique individuals. I ask both groups of my students to write about what they care about, what they know about—what they are experts in.

As the students in the Alternative High School have begun to abandon their notions of "academic" writing, and reached into their own experiences and feelings for their material, they have begun to succeed in a way that they never believed they could. When Mark moved from writing a maximum of two sentences a day, to writing a four-page piece about his deer hunting trip, and the kill he made, we both succeeded. He had made a leap into believing that something that he knew and felt could be worthwhile for another person to read about; his self-esteem soared. His sense that he was interesting and capable and worthwhile translated directly into the attitude he brought to his other school work, and he began to excel academically in a way that he had not since the second grade (he is 18 years old now). The patience and encouragement with which I responded to his first tentative efforts at writing something that mattered *to him* paid off for me as a teacher. Not only did he begin to succeed in a much more traditional way as a student—he began to feel his worth as a human being.

This connection between writing and self-esteem is a very powerful one. By giving students constant positive feedback, I can help their confidence to soar. And when their confidence is high, they can achieve far more than if they feel ignorant, and stupid, and incapable. Because writing about what we know and care about is such an intimately personal act, it can only succeed in an atmosphere that respects the individual, and nurtures that which is unique in each person. A logical outcome of a nurturing environment in which respect for personhood is paramount is that both good writing and self-esteem flourish.[1]

This way of thinking about the teaching of writing has gotten its contemporary impetus from the work of Lucy Calkins at Teachers College, Columbia University. It is generally referred to as "writing process" theory and practice. Here are some quotations from her book, *The Art of Teaching Writing.*

Human beings have a deep need to represent their experience through writing. . . . There is no plot line in the bewildering complexity of our lives but that which we make and find ourselves. By articulating experience, we reclaim it for ourselves. . . . We write because we want to understand our lives.

I know that teaching writing begins with the recognition that each individual comes to the writing workshop with concerns, ideas, memories, and feelings. Our job as teachers is to listen and to help them listen. "What are the things you know and care about?" I ask writers, and I ask this whether the writers are five years old or fifty.

When writing becomes a personal project for children, teachers are freed from cajoling, pushing, pulling, and motivating. The teaching act changes. With a light touch we can guide and extend children's growth in writing. Also, our teaching becomes more personal, and this makes all the difference in the world.[2]

Given what you now know of the therapist approach, what is your reaction to it? Opposed? Favorable? Are you wondering whether you might be something of the executive, doing an effective job of getting students to learn school subjects, while also being part therapist, encouraging them to come to grips with what they are as human beings? Can you be both? Unfortunately, it does not appear that we are permitted to combine these two approaches, for they rest on very different conceptions of what it means to be a person. A brief look at the social and psychological foundations of the therapist approach will explain the logical proscription against using the two approaches together.

Roots in Social Criticism

In the previous chapter, we mentioned Lyndon Johnson's Great Society programs and the Coleman Report. Just before that era, education in the United States was making its closing adjustment to the great educational debate of the thirties and forties, traditional versus progressive education. As educational institutions sought an accommodation to progressive educational ideals, while remaining essentially traditional in structure and purpose, the Soviet Union launched *Sputnik*, President Kennedy was assassinated, President Johnson advocated both guns and butter (meaning the nation could both fight the war in Vietnam and still support massive social justice programs), and our national awareness of the tight connections between schooling and equal opportunity for members of different racial and cultural groups increased dramatically. In the midst of this social and political unease, a number of educational theories were advanced.

The therapist approach was one of these theories. It arose from a fascinating conjunction of contemporary social criticism and a new version of psychology developed in opposition to behaviorism and experimental methods. In England, A. S. Neill had founded and successfully run Summerhill, a school where students were free to choose to attend class or not and even to decide if they wanted to learn to read or do math.[3] In the United States, Paul Goodman was one of the harshest and most read of the social critics. His *Growing Up Absurd* had the force of holy writ for the sixties counterculture.[4] Goodman's most pungent criticisms of education, however, are not in *Growing Up Absurd*, but in *Compulsory Mis-Education*[5] and in the many articles he wrote for magazines and journals. Writing for the *Saturday Review* in 1968, he strongly endorsed the view that we can "educate the young entirely in terms of their free choice, with no processing whatever. Nothing can be efficiently learned, or, indeed, learned at all . . . unless it meets need, desire, curiosity, or fantasy."[6]

In what seems like a direct swipe at the executive approach, Goodman argued, "It seems stupid to decide a priori what the young ought to know and then try to motivate them, instead of letting the initiative come from them and putting information and relevant equipment at their service."[7] The typical rejoinder to this contention was to point out that this way of educating the young may not be in best interests of the society in the long run. To which Goodman replied:

> If the young, as they mature, can follow their bent and choose their topics, times, and teachers, and if teachers teach what they themselves consider important—which is all they can skillfully teach anyway—the needs of society will be adequately met; there will be more lively, independent, and inventive people; and in the fairly short run there will be a more sensible and efficient society.[8]

At the time, this proposal was considered radical; it still is. Notice that Goodman gives a central role to choice for the learner. The learner chooses the content to be learned, when and how it is to be learned, and who is to teach it. The teacher's obligation in this setting is to enhance the learner's power to choose and to help the student use what is learned as an opportunity for personal growth. Herbert Kohl, another prominent advocate for alternative forms of education in the 1960s, comments on the teacher's role as an example in the life of the learner:

Of course the teacher is a moral exemplar—an example of all the confusion, hypocrisy, and indecision, of all the mistakes, as well as the triumphs, of moral man. The children see all this, whatever they pretend to see. Therefore, to be more than an example, to be an educator—someone capable of helping lead the child through the labyrinth of life—the teacher must be honest to the children about his mistakes and weaknesses; he must be able to say that he is wrong or sorry. . . . It is the teacher's struggle to be moral that excites his pupils; it is honesty, not rightness, that moves children.[9]

Humanistic Psychology

Many of the educational ideas coming from these social critics were rooted in an alternative psychology known as humanistic or "third-force" psychology. Gordon Allport, Abraham Maslow, and Carl Rogers were among the leading figures in this school of psychology. Each of these psychologists stresses the uniqueness of individuals, and the difficulties that psychology, in its attempts to become a science of mind or behavior, has had in treating the individual with proper regard for his or her unique properties.

Maslow does not deny the behaviorist contention that individuals act in response to stimuli, but he argues that this action must be understood as the result of an interaction between the person's needs and the unique "lifespace" of every person. Each one of us has a hierarchy of drives from basic survival needs for food and water to such higher-level needs as to give and receive love, to develop self-esteem, and to appreciate beauty. A person who interprets his situation effectively and thereby meets his needs to the highest level possible for his lifespace is, according to Maslow, a self-actualized person. A fully self-actualized person is one who possesses a balanced and integrated personality, with such positive traits as autonomy, creativeness, independence, altruism, and a healthy goal-directedness.[10]

The goals of self-actualization and authenticity are quite compatible with one another. The teacher as therapist seeks both, insofar as he or she strives to develop students with healthy personalities, able to plan, choose, and act in ways that advance their own educational growth and development. Although many educators have embraced Maslow's notion of self-actualization, Maslow did not develop its implications for education. It is to the work of Carl Rogers that we must turn for the pedagogical implications of humanistic psychology.

"Teaching," claims Rogers, "is a vastly over-rated function."[11] "It is most unfortunate that educators and the public think about, and focus on, *teaching*. It leads them into a host of questions which are either irrelevant or absurd so far as real education is concerned."[12] He bases this view of teaching on the importance of what he calls "experiential learning." This is learning that is filled with personal involvement; the whole person is *in* the learning event, not a passive absorber of whatever the teacher dispenses. It is learning that is self-initiated. It is pervasive; it influences every aspect of the learner's being. It is evaluated by the learner, not by the teacher or by tests. It is rooted in meaning, which is to say that the learning has personal meaning for the learner; it advances the learner's power to understand and influence events that are important in his or her life.

Learning of this kind cannot be controlled by a teacher. It must be freely engaged in by the learner. The teacher can only guide, suggest, encourage, and maybe even, when the occasion is appropriate, warn. Rogers believes that "anything that can be taught to another is relatively inconsequential and has little or no significant influence on behavior."[13] What is important is not what can be taught, but rather what is learned. "The only learning which significantly influences behavior is self-discovered, self-appropriated learning." This self-discovered learning constitutes truth that is "personally appropriated and assimilated in experience."[14] Because learning of this type is *personally* appropriated, it "cannot be directly communicated to another."[15] Thus the teacher is not one who imparts knowledge and skill to another, but one who helps another gain his own knowledge and skill. In the role of guide or facilitator, the teacher must be "a real person in his relationship with his students. He can be enthusiastic, he can be bored, he can be interested in students, he can be angry, he can be sensitive and sympathetic. Because he accepts these feelings as his own he has no need to impose them on his students."[16]

Humanistic psychology, as Maslow and Rogers make quite evident, is a psychology based on freedom, choice, personal growth, and the development of emotional and mental health. In their view, education makes a significant contribution to these ends, but not by the traditional mechanisms of packaging subject-matter content for delivery to student learners. Instead, the student must be helped to attain his or her own realization. The teacher's task is to direct the learner inward, toward the self, so that the learner is thereby enabled to reach outward, choosing the content to be acquired and the actions that follow from mastery of this content. This relationship between teacher and student has been described by Noddings and Shore as one of intuitive caring and loving. They call it *educational caritas*, "the sense of caring and intuitive sensitivity between teacher and student, the love and intuitive 'feel' for a subject area that may be felt by both teacher and student, and love for the act of learning and teaching."[17]

What is your view on being an executive and a therapist? Can you do both? Not if you accept Rogers's argument. He contends that you cannot put knowledge in someone's head (not in any way that is meaningful), as the executive approach would have you do. Any attempt at teaching in the executive manner will diminish the learners, keeping them from appropriating and assimilating that knowledge in their own experience and thus keeping them from realizing the meaning and the freedom that leads to living an authentic and self-actualized life. To the therapist teacher, the executive approach leads to alienation by driving a wedge between the knower and the known. When the teacher becomes the executive, the learners always acquire someone else's knowledge, on someone else's terms, for someone else's purposes. There seems no compromise possible here, no way to have the cake of the therapist and eat it as an executive.

Is there really no way to bridge the gap? It seems not. Recall that the executive approach is grounded in a behavioristic, experimental psychology, which itself is grounded in the philosophy of logical empiricism or positivism. Positivism is a philosophical position regarding knowledge that elevates to the highest levels of regard observation in the natural world, public testability of hypotheses, objectivity, and verifiability of claims. It was most fully developed in the late nineteenth century. In a somewhat modified, contemporary version, positivism provides the sustaining concepts for our modern view of science and a highly quantitative form of educational research. The languages of purpose and freedom, of feelings and emotions, of intuition and caring, and of subjective and spiritual experience that are important to the humanistic psychologist are generally *verboten* in the positivist-behaviorist world. However, newer forms of educational research, often called "qualitative research," have challenged positivism and try to bring more of the human dimension of education into the purview of researchers. Nevertheless, the fundamental opposition and incompatibility of these views seems to be irresolvable.

Existentialism

In contrast to positivism, the undergirding philosophy for humanistic psychology is existentialism. In the minds of many, positivism and existentialism are archenemies. It would take us far afield to explore existentialism in any depth, but we can touch on just enough to complete the description of the therapist approach to teaching. One of the few tenets that existentialists hold in common is that existence precedes essence; that we simply are before we are anything in particular. One of the best known existentialists, Jean-Paul Sartre, explains:

> What do we mean by saying that existence precedes essence? We mean that man first of all exists, encounters himself, surges up in the world—and defines himself afterwards. If man as the existentialist sees him is not definable, it is because to begin with he is nothing. He will not be anything until later, and then he will be what he makes of himself. . . . Man is nothing else but that which he makes of himself. That is the first principle of existentialism.[18]

We become something as we confront the world and choose our way through it. If we avoid these choices and their consequences, then we are, in fact, avoiding what is the essence of being human: our freedom. It was Sartre who wrote of persons fleeing from their freedom. They did so because absolute, total freedom is so frightening. It is hard to confront the view that we may do differently anything we are now doing; that we can always choose to act another way, think a different thought, feel a new emotion. Yet to be authentic, we must confront our freedom, we must create meaning for ourselves, and we must choose our way to and through our future.

Do you recall our example of Jim Barnes teaching a math unit to his fifth grade? He wants his students to learn the formula for computing the area of plane surfaces bounded by straight lines. Note that he has in mind some x, a formula for computing area, that he wants to get across to his *Ss*. He is an executive-type teacher who follows the curriculum guide, and thus mathematics is what is covered in this class. Most students are in his classroom because they are assigned to it. Jim would, of course, be delighted if his students took a sustaining interest in mathematics, and he will try many tricks and ploys to gain their interest. But in the end, say the humanistic psychologist and the existentialist, it will come to nothing. The students did not choose to learn about computing area. There is little in their lives that would lead them to personally appropriate and assimilate this knowledge. Jim Barnes is not charged with the responsibility for, nor is he really interested in, enhancing the capacities of his students to choose, to gain in personal identity, and to enlarge their sense of power and meaning.

What do you think of Jim Barnes? Is he damaging the minds and stunting the psyches of his students? Or is he legitimately pursuing an effective approach to teaching? Whatever you might think at this moment, is it clear why there is a problem with trying to be both executive and therapist, at least at the same time? Perhaps you are considering being an executive on some occasions and a therapist on others. To which the existentialist might scream, "You either believe that students should be presented with the content to be learned, or that they can and should determine their own learning. You either believe that a teacher can teach some specific content to a learner, or that the teacher can only guide the learner in the pursuit of specific content. You believe that the purpose of education is either to instruct the learner in knowledge and skill, or to engender authenticity and self-actualization. CHOOSE! You cannot sit on the fence. You cannot do both."

Afterthoughts

If you are befuddled by this problem, pulled in two directions, you are not alone. The split between the positivist-behavioristic and the existentialist-humanistic approaches is one of the classic antagonisms in modern philosophy and psychology. Walter Kaufmann states the disjunction well:

> It is one of the saddest features of our age that we are faced with an entirely unnecessary dichotomy: on the one hand there are those whose devotion to intellectual cleanliness and rigor is exemplary but who refuse to deal with anything but small, and often downright trivial, questions; in the other camp are men like Toynbee and some of the existentialists who deal with the big and interesting questions, but in such a manner that the positivists point to them as living proofs that any effort of this kind is doomed to failure. Aware of their opponents' errors, both sides go to ever greater extremes; the split widens; and the intelligent layman who is left in the middle will soon lose sight of both.[19]

In education, we seem to be caught in the same bind. There have been many attempts to describe teaching in cause-and-effect, process-product, positivistic terminology, but the critics say this leaves out the genuinely human dimension that makes teaching meaningful. We have also had phenomenological and existential descriptions of teaching as unique personal experiences, but the critics say that we cannot draw useful generalizations from such personal narrative accounts. Can you effect a resolution of your own, something that will enable you to use both therapist and executive approaches in the classroom? We have not left you with much hope for doing so, have we?

While you ponder these questions, there is a small detail that we would like to clean up. While discussing the therapist's approach to the

Educated-Person card, we stated that advocates of this approach to teaching would strongly oppose any such card. Why? Because each person is unique. As each person chooses his or her way into a self-projected future, that uniqueness is maintained. Thus there is no shared standard or common outcome that can be used to determine when someone qualifies for the E-P card. There is no specialized knowledge here that is certifiable by a College Board test or a Graduate Record Examination. You could, perhaps, choose to award an E-P card to yourself, but why would you want such a thing? It would not mean anything to anyone else, inasmuch as you awarded it to yourself on the basis of your own uniqueness.

And herein lies a difficult problem for the therapist approach to teaching. Each person is unique. This uniqueness is maintained by making choices. You must make the choices on the basis of the future you construct for yourself. But what of the future of others? What of the future of the community? The state? The nation? May not these entities exercise jurisdiction over schooling in order to ensure some common meaning and serve common purposes? Should not the government of the people impose a shared program of studies on each child in order to preserve the culture and the nation?

In the United States it has long been accepted that the maintenance of democracy and national identity requires a common education. This is generally made manifest as a common core of studies for all students. Once this core is acquired, then students may usually select from a range of programs and courses or, if old enough, leave school altogether. But first, the common good must be considered. How, then, are we to tolerate the students' choosing the time, place, and content of their education, as the therapist approach would have it?

Again, your desire, like ours, may be to look for compromise. The therapist approach is so attractive, so filled with dignity and hope for each human being, that we resist letting go of it. But, as we have asked before, how can you have both and be at all consistent with the principles and imperatives of either approach? Everything about each approach says, "Choose!" What will you do?

Before trying to decide the issue, we would like you to consider the cases and disputes that table 1 links to the therapist approach. You will find these in chapter 6. Then we will examine one more approach. It is not a compromise approach, nor is it some sort of resolution of the paradox that behaviorism and humanism pose. This third approach places great emphasis on the x in $T\phi Sxy$ and comes out looking quite different from either of the approaches considered thus far in terms of both ϕ and y.

Chapter 4

The Liberationist Approach

The two approaches examined thus far stress different variables in the $T\phi Sxy$ formula. The executive approach highlights what the teacher does (ϕ). The therapist approach emphasizes what the student (S) is and chooses to become. The approaches each have different purposes (which appear to be mutually exclusive, given the arguments just sketched). The executive teacher strives for the learner's acquisition of specified knowledge and skill. The therapist teacher supports and guides the learner in becoming an authentic person. We have considered every variable in the formula save one. Though x has been mentioned often, it has not been featured until now. The liberationist approach to teaching brings content, x, to the forefront.

A Case Study

To illustrate the liberationist approach, we would again like you to imagine yourself a teacher. This time you have just completed college with a double major in math and physics. You are very proud of that achievement, and even prouder that you turned down several job offers with private industry because you want to be a teacher. You have long regretted what you regard as the poor preparation secondary students receive in math and the natural sciences. You love these fields and look forward to sharing your knowledge with your students. You have your pick of schools; preparation like yours is not an everyday occurrence for beginning teachers. You select a fine high school in a middle-class, racially mixed suburban community.

You have five periods, two of physics and three of math. One physics class is advanced placement (AP), the other is general physics for students contemplating college. One math course is pre-algebra, the other two are algebra I classes. You prepare extensively for these courses, supplementing the textbooks with workbooks, your own custom-made supporting materials, and a full range of visual aids, including colorful charts and graphs, posters, slides, filmstrips, even a few movies depicting famous scientists and mathematicians struggling with the great intellectual problems of their times.

In each course, your interest is that as many students as possible will confront the material in the way a physicist or mathematician might. For example, you decide to begin the unit on electricity simply, by using a flashlight or ordinary house lamp as a starting point. But before the first period of that lesson is over, you plan to consider circuits, polarity, resistance, and current flow. From there you will introduce the basic mathematics typically used in electrical computations, and then the atomic character of electrical and electronic circuits. Along the way, you will introduce the students to Gilbert, Faraday, Maxwell, and Neumann. By the end of the unit, you hope to have covered conduction, resonance, filtration, and magnetic effects, as well as thermal and biochemical effects.

How do you plan to teach all this content? That troubles you a bit, but not excessively. You know the material well. You feel certain you can bring it alive for the students through careful use of instructional aids, through historical and biographical sketches, and by involving the students in exercises and experiments that bring them face-to-face with problems to be solved. You are concerned about how to communicate this complex material to classes containing a range of different students—different abilities, different experiences, different interests—although here again you are not overly troubled. You are confident of the value of your material for the students and are prepared to make adjustments as you learn about their differences.

Features of This Approach

This heavy emphasis on content, with much less emphasis on specific teaching skills or the psychic and emotional states of your students, makes you a candidate for the liberationist approach. But only a candidate. Full membership requires consideration of the purpose of teaching beyond the emphasis on content, just as consideration of purpose is essential to the therapist and executive approaches. Mere emphasis on the student does not make you a therapist; you must focus on the student for the purpose of helping him become authentic. Mere emphasis on the technical skills of teaching does not make you an executive; you must also seek the student's effective acquisition of specific knowledge and skill. Mere emphasis on content does not make you a liberationist; you must aim at freeing the student's mind from the limits of everyday experience, from the deadness and banality of convention and stereotype. Thus the content of your physics and math classes must be selected and organized for the particular purpose of liberating the mind of the student.

You might object at this point, saying that so far you cannot tell the difference between x in the executive approach and x in the liberationist approach. Both deal with knowledge, and both appear to deal with specific knowledge, although the liberationist approach appears to describe that knowledge at a high level of sophistication. But surely mere differences in depth and scope of knowledge cannot be the only things separating the executive x from the liberationist x. If that is your retort, take a bow. You are right on target.

The nature of the knowledge and the way it is explored are different in the executive and liberationist approaches. The x in the executive approach is, as we pointed out earlier, highly specified. It is made up of discrete facts, ideas, topics, and domains, often expressed in the form of behavioral outcomes or measurable competencies. This kind of tight specification is required if objective, standardized tests are to be used to determine what, if anything, the learners gained from their teachers. Recall that the teacher's task is to move x from its source to the mind of the learner. The manner of this instruction seems quite determined by those technical skills of teaching that have been proven effective for producing gains in specified knowledge.

In the liberationist approach, the manner of instruction is heavily influenced by the content itself. For example, as a science teacher, you hope your students will become critical, skeptical inquirers, because that is a prerequisite mindset for doing good science. In order for the students to learn to think in this way, they must see it being done (it is unlikely that it will be learned from reading the text). *You* are the teacher who must serve as the model for the students. If you wish them to become critical inquirers, as the nature of your subject demands, they must observe you doing critical inquiry. To model it, you often have to *do* science in your classroom, so that they can see what it means for them to do science as critical inquirers. It is nonsense for you to expect them to behave critically and questioningly about phenomena in the world when the person who teaches the subject does not act that way.

Manner in Teaching

This way of acting as a teacher is called "manner." Not the "manner" of "table manners" (though akin to it), but the "manner" of "I like his manner." A manner is a relatively stable disposition to act in a given way under circumstances that call for such action. We speak of persons who are gentle, humorous, affectionate, secretive, ambitious. These words describe their manner. Under appropriate circumstances, an affectionate person will smile, touch, hug, offer support, and ask sympathetic questions, while the same circumstances might lead a person of shy manner to become quiet, frown, and pull away.

The manner of the teacher is critical to the liberationist approach, for it determines, in large measure, whether the knowledge and skill to be learned will free the mind or simply trap it with dull and irrelevant facts and skills. One of the foremost contemporary advocates for the liberationist approach, R. S. Peters, illuminates the idea of manner as he discusses what he calls "principles of procedure" for teaching such subjects as science or history:

> There must be respect for evidence and a ban on "cooking" or distorting it; there must be a willingness to admit that one is mistaken; there must be non-interference with people who wish to put forward objections; there must be a respect for people as a source of argument and an absence of personal invective and contempt for what they say because of who they are. To learn science is not just to learn facts and to understand theories; it is also to learn to participate in a public form of life governed by such principles of procedure. Insofar, therefore, as a person is educated scientifically, he will have to absorb these principles of procedure by means of which the content of scientific thought has been accumulated and is criticized and developed.[1]

These principles of procedure are part of what we mean by manner. Note that Peters speaks of showing respect for evidence and for people as a source of argument; of not interfering during the presentation of alternatives; of not using invective and showing contempt for different views. These are manners (consistent ways of behaving) that the teacher must display in order to teach science well. The teacher must not only display these manners, but call attention to and encourage their imitation by students and give praise when students exhibit these manners themselves. It is not enough for the liberationist that knowledge and skill are simply acquired, no matter how fully or completely. They must be acquired in a manner appropriate to the kind of knowledge it is.

In the teaching of literature, for instance, the manner of instruction might be somewhat different from that of science. Here the teacher might wish to exhibit and encourage passion and involvement, while the teaching of science calls for dispassion and detachment. In art and music, the teacher might show disregard for the conventional rules of harmony, balance, rhythm, or color in order to encourage creative expression in the medium, whereas it is only under very special conditions that the scientist may disregard the methodological rules of conventional scientific inquiry. Each major subject field typically has a set of manners, principles of procedures as Peters call them, appropriate to that field.

If we have described the idea of manner with sufficient clarity, we can add a little complexity to this discussion without throwing you off stride. Not only is the manner of teaching influenced by the *nature* of the content (for example, physics, literature, or art), it is also influenced by the *sophistication* of the content. If the content is undeveloped and low level, what value and fascination could possibly accompany such content? Unsophisticated content gives the teacher little range and depth of manner. This situation might be compared to an actress faced with a poor script. She does not want to play it because it will not challenge her thespian talent; it denies her range and depth.

The specified knowledge so valued in the executive approach is especially subject to this shortcoming. The knowledge and skills are so highly specified in order that the learner's accumulated fund of knowledge and skill can be diagnosed accurately, an instructional prescription prepared, instruction given, and, finally, an unambiguous evaluation administered. The difficulty is that knowledge and skill are specified at so basic and detailed a level that it becomes impossible for the teacher to impart it in a manner that reflects anything but a rudimentary, sometimes even primitive, approach to the content. This outcome is much less likely in the liberationist approach because there is a strong emphasis on sophisticated content.

Moral and Intellectual Virtues

We will look more carefully at this notion of sophistication in a moment. Right now there is one detail about manner that needs to be added. We discussed manner that is specific to subject fields and how this manner is affected by the sophistication with which the content is developed for the classroom. There is also what might be called general manner. Its form and character are not dependent on the different fields; it is applicable across all fields. This general manner is usually grouped under the heading of "moral and intellectual virtues." Among the moral virtues are honesty, integrity, fair mindedness, and just treatment. Among the intellectual virtues are reasonableness, openmindedness, regard for evidence, curiosity, a reflective habit of mind, and judicious skepticism.

Each of these denotes a manner of behaving that the liberationist would insist be characteristic of all teaching. Indeed, these moral and intellectual virtues are considered part of the content of the liberationist approach. They are to be acquired by the learner just as the knowledge and skill in the subject field are to be acquired. Whoops! Did you catch that? We have been rolling along here speaking of manner and content as if they were two different entities, and now we just said that manner is part of the content. Take a moment. See if you can sort this out on your own. Then come back to the text.

Manner is part of the content of instruction because all the time you are imparting the content of some subject to the students, you are also imparting the way you approach and deal with that content. Students learn not only from what you say and assign to them, they learn from the way you do it. Typically you might not think much about this facet of teaching (it is part of what is meant by the notion of "hidden curriculum"), but to the liberationist it is a vital part of instruction. The liberationist wants the student to acquire the manner (general and special) as well as the content, for the content without the manner will not be liberating.

Traits of Character

It may be hard to see how manner becomes part of content, because it cannot be taught to students directly, as can knowledge, skills, and understanding. These latter outcomes are achieved through a kind of frontal attack. But there is another type of learning outcome, called "traits of character." It differs from the other three because it is difficult to approach directly. It sounds a bit silly for a teacher to say, "Today I am going to teach you kindness," although it does not sound silly to say, "Today I am going to teach you the Pythagorean theorem," or "I am going to teach you how an atomic reaction is initiated and sustained." Traits of character are taught through example and model, not by direct instruction. As such, they must be part of the manner of the teacher if they are to be acquired by the learner. However, even though they are taught indirectly, they are still very much a part of what the liberationist teacher wants the student to learn. This feature is what makes manner part of content. The British philosopher Gilbert Ryle, looking at such traits as hard work and fair mindedness, offers a helpful description:

> What will help to make us self-controlled, fair-minded or hard-working are good examples set by others, and then ourselves practising and failing, and practising again, and failing again, but not quite so soon and so on. In matters of morals, as in the skills and arts, we learn first by being shown by others, then by being trained by others, naturally with some worded homily, praise and rebuke, and lastly by being trained by ourselves.[2]

Ryle contends that we learn traits of character by being shown and trained, with encouragement or reprimand, as appropriate. We master the trait by finally training ourselves to live it well. This is the way the student aquires manner from the teacher. The well-known child psychologist Urie Bronfenbrenner makes a similar point:

> However important genetic factors may be in the determination of human behavior, it is quite clear that such qualities as mutual trust, kindness, cooperation, and social responsibility cannot be insured through selective breeding; they are learned from other human beings who in some measure exhibit these qualities, value them, and strive to develop them in their children. It is a matter of social rather than biological inheritance. Or, as one of the author's teachers, Walter Fenno Dearborn, used to put it: "He's a chip off the old block—not because he was knocked off it, but because he knocked around with it."[3]

There is little that is more destructive of the liberationist approach than calling for a manner from students that is neither possessed nor exemplified by the teacher. Each of us has had teachers of this kind: the science teacher who asks for critical thinking from students, but never veers from the problem sets in the text or the answers in the teacher's edition; the art teacher who talks incessantly about being creative and expressive, but always structures the assignment and has rigorous standards for neatness in the art room; the elementary school teacher who admonishes students to share, but yells when anyone forgets a pencil or touches any of his materials on the back table.

The liberationist teacher is careful to serve as a model for the special and general manner required to free the mind of the learner from dogma, convention, and stereotype. If creativity is required, this teacher does not teach a unit on creativity; creativity is not so much a skill to be taught directly as it is a way to approach tasks and activities. So the teacher acts creatively, calling on students to follow the lead and offering the opportunity and safety for them to try being creative. The same is true for critical thinking, for compassion, and for fair play. These and many other key traits are acquired indirectly from instruction that also aims at imparting knowledge, skill, and understanding.

Forms of Knowledge

A while ago we distinguished the nature of the content studied from the level of sophistication at which the content is developed and presented to students. We promised to return to this point after discussing manner. It is time to do so. Remember that content in the executive approach is highly specified, as it must be if the teacher as executive is to function well. These demands on content stem primarily from past experience with what kind of content children are most likely to master, plus the requirement that this content be developed so that it can be assessed accurately at a later time. The demands of the liberationist approach are quite different. A teacher inclined toward the liberationist approach believes that the mind can only be developed and freed by the acquisition of a broad range of fundamental knowledge and understanding, combined with the most fitting intellectual and moral traits of character. What is included in the category of "fundamental knowledge and understanding" must not be determined simply by what children are most likely to learn successfully or by what can be tested with the greatest reliability and validity.

The liberationist places some strict controls on what counts as knowledge and understanding, and thus on what is proper to the curriculum. One of the most thorough contemporary explications of these controls has been put forward by P. H. Hirst.[4] He argues that knowledge can be divided into seven forms. They are mathematics, physical sciences, human sciences, history, religion, literature and fine arts, and philosophy. Hirst states that these seven forms or domains cover all the kinds of things we as human beings can come to know about in the world. The best education is the one that initiates students into these forms of knowledge.

In addition to a concern for *what* the proper forms of knowledge are, the liberationist also places stipulations on *how* the forms should be taught. That is, you can neither pick just any topic for instruction (you must, if your goal is to free the mind, select from among the forms) nor approach it any way you please. For Hirst, a form of knowledge has some special characteristics that can help the liberationist teacher see what is fundamental and what is mind building about a subject. A form of knowledge is a coherent conceptual system that humankind has collectively developed over time to make sense of particular areas of human experience. Each form has its own special concepts that capture key aspects of human experience.

For example, to make sense of artistic experiences, we need a concept of beauty; to make sense of experiences in the natural, physical world, we need such concepts as truth, fact, and evidence; and to understand mathematical phenomena, we need the concept of number. Besides these key concepts, each form of knowledge, according to Hirst, has a distinctive logical structure of its own (think of the difference between the rules for solving equations in math and the rules of grammar in a language), a set of special skills and methods for making knowledge claims in that form (think of scientific method), and a set of unique standards for publicly testing and judging claims (think of literary or artistic criticism).

These notions may seem excessively complex. One reason some of us have difficulty grasping them is that we have not, ourselves, had many teachers who fully understood and were committed to the liberationist approach. Thus we find it hard to assimilate liberationist notions into our own experiences with education. For this reason, it might be helpful to simplify some of the ideas just covered. We will try not to do violence to these concepts by transforming them into somewhat more ordinary ideas and metaphors, but it would be a good idea if you reread the material of the last few pages after you finish the next few paragraphs.

As we grow and develop, we experience the world around us. Information and data come into our heads through our senses. We listen, see, feel, hear, and taste things in the world. We can do several things with what enters our heads. We can, in a manner of speaking, toss it right back out (forget it or ignore it). We can store it for a short period of time and not give much thought to it. We can ponder it, wonder about it, and even do something about it. We can elaborate on it, connect it with some other things, and perhaps create new information or ideas. Of course, everything that happens inside our heads has an influence on the information that we continue to gain through our senses. What we know and feel about our world can have a profound impact on what we will look and listen for, what we will see, and how we will interpret what we see, feel, and hear.

Let us call all this entering information and data "input." How we filter, process, and structure this input is a critical matter to the liberationist. The forms of knowledge mentioned above are considered to be among the very finest means for imparting structure to experience—for giving experience profound and useful meaning and for empowering us to control and mediate our experience. These forms of knowledge are not comprised simply of facts, figures, and formulae; they are key or central ideas, distinctive logical structures, methods of inquiry, and publicly held standards of judgment. If we learn these latter characteristics of the forms while we learn the facts, figures, and formulae, then we have truly made knowledge the basis for freeing the mind from the limits, deceptions, and conventionality of ordinary, unstructured experience.

A teacher might consider himself a liberationist if he stresses content, the x in $T\phi Sxy$. However, if the content is seen merely as facts, figures, and formulae, the teacher is not a liberationist, even though x seems to be the emphasized variable in that person's instruction. Remember that in addition to imparting subject-area content, the liberationist teacher must also exemplify the manner of a liberally educated person; he or she must possess and model the moral and intellectual virtues we discussed earlier. Now there is another wrinkle: The content itself must be developed in particular ways. It must be planned and presented so that the learner can grasp the root structure of the various forms of knowledge, and in this way the learner is enabled to structure his or her own experience.

The structure of the content is, according to Hirst and many other educational theorists, revealed by attending to the key concepts of a given form, its distinctive logical structures (the rules and heuristics that govern the way concepts and knowledge claims connect), its methods for undertaking formal inquiry (such as scientific method, historiography, ethnography, or phenomenology), and its standards for testing and judging hypotheses or claims. Thus, to acquire a discipline (physics, chemistry, history, psychology, and so forth) is to learn its major ideas, understand its logical structure, be able to undertake controlled inquiry within its domain of experience, and know what determines the merit and worth of your findings or productions.

The notion that knowledge has a form or structure has long been a part of liberationist thinking. It received a great deal of attention in the curriculum development movement of the 1960s, spurred on by the now-classic book by Jerome S. Bruner, *The Process of Education*. Bruner wrote that "grasping the structure of a subject is understanding it in a way that permits many other things to be related to it meaningfully. To learn structure, in short, is to learn how things are related."[5] Bruner then discussed the importance of key ideas:

> The basic ideas that lie at the heart of all science and mathematics and the basic themes that give form to life and literature are as simple as they are powerful. To be in command of these basic ideas, to use them effectively, requires a continual deepening of one's understanding of them that comes from learning to use them in progressively more complex forms.[6]

It is not surprising that we would draw on Bruner to help us describe the nature of content in the liberationist approach. He is a cognitive psychologist and, as such, represents a different school of thought from the behaviorism of the executive approach and the humanistic psychology of the therapist approach. Because the cognitive psychologist is especially interested in the way we acquire, interpret, apply, and expand our knowledge, there is a close affiliation between the liberationist and the cognitive psychologist. However, it would be an error to press this point too far, for the liberationist approach is not nearly so rooted in psychology (of any kind) as the executive and therapist approaches. The parentage of the liberationist approach is more philosophical. To the extent that this approach would call upon psychology for assistance, however, cognitive psychology would be the preferred school of thought.

Liberation as Emancipation

There is another recent thrust of liberationist thinking coming out of neo-Marxist philosophy that is more political and social in orientation than it is subject-matter and manner focused. Here we will treat it as a variant of the liberationist approach because it aims to free the mind in a special way, but there are some educators who would argue that it is a distinct approach in its own right. They would call it critical pedagogy or emancipationist teaching. The emancipationist sees the social world as a place of constant struggle and oppression where those who have power, privilege, and status assert themselves and those who perceive themselves as lesser persons accept their fate and powerlessness. The emancipationists argue that schools are instruments of social reproduction in which the lower classes learn to be docile workers who follow orders and the upper classes are trained for leadership and the exercise of power. The point (y) of emancipationist teaching, then, is to free the minds of students from the unconscious grip of oppressive ideas about their class, gender, race, or ethnic status because these ideas imprison them, debilitate them, and cut them off from their chances for a better life.

Perhaps the best-known, early articulator of the role of the emancipationist teacher is Paulo Freire, the Brazilian educator who developed a method for teaching illiterate adult peasants in the backward northeastern region of Brazil. He was exiled for his work in 1964. His book *Pedagogy of the Oppressed*[7] presents his political and philosophical ideas as well as the pedagogical practices he has developed to stimulate and sustain *"critical consciousness"* in people.

Freire's fundamental concern is with the liberation of poor, powerless, and ignorant people who have been subject to slavelike domination by wealthy people. He believes that an oppressive view of social reality is imposed by the dominant groups on the oppressed, making it impossible for the oppressed to perceive and assess their situation or even to think it can be otherwise. This version of social reality is inculcated through words, images, customs, myths, popular culture, and in countless obvious and subtle ways that pervade public life. The oppressed accept this version as reality and are psychologically devastated by it. By accepting the dominant view, they come to think of themselves as worthless, helpless, and inferior. They acquire the personality traits characteristic of oppressed people: fatalism, self-deprecation, and emotional dependence.

The primary task of education, for Freire, is to overcome these attitudes and replace them with traits of active freedom and human responsibility. This cannot be done by treating the oppressed as objects whose behaviors are to be transformed by the teacher. Rather, they must be treated as active human agents who deserve our help, so that they can achieve their own liberation. They need to be awakened "to see themselves as men engaged in the ontological and historical vocation of becoming more fully human."[8] This is to be accomplished through dialogue. The task of the teacher as emancipator is problem posing—"posing of the problems of men in their relations with the world."[9] The students and their teacher must become collaborators, co-investigators developing together their consciousness of reality and their images of a possible, better reality. This ability to step back from an unconscious acceptance of things as they are and to perceive the world critically, even in the midst of pervasive, powerful, subtle forces tending to distort and oppress, is what Freire means by attaining *critical consciousness*.

In the United States in more recent times, the work of Michael Apple, Henry Giroux, Peter McClaren, Stanley Aronowitz, Thomas Popkewitz, Ira Shor, and others[10] has carried forward the emancipationist stance against the evils of social reproduction.

For these emancipationist theorists, the aim of education is raising the critical consciousness of the oppressed so they can free themselves from a life of domination by others. They believe that this is the proper aim for the education not only of the peasants of Brazil, but also of the poor and the oppressed in large cities, of migrant workers, of factory workers in all parts of the world, and of all anywhere who have learned not to question their lot in life. Some of the current efforts in multicultural education, black and women's studies, and bilingual programs are examples of the emancipationist program. While both the emancipationist and the liberationist seek to free the minds of students, the goals of the emancipationist are unashamedly political. Both, however, seek a moral end for education, the freedom of the mind. In an effort to distinguish the two, we will use the term "emancipationist" to refer to the educational programs argued for by those who embrace the ideas of Freire and others. The term "liberationist" is reserved for those who represent the more mainstream notions of liberal education, such as manner, virtue, forms of knowledge, and *paideia*.

The Paideia Proposal

We have already noted that the liberationist approach is rooted much more deeply in philosophy than psychology. These roots may be traced back to Plato and Aristotle. In a sense, the notion of liberal education is decidedly Greek. Philosophers still turn to the works of Greeks (and such Romans as Horace, Virgil, and Cicero) for the basic premises of liberal education. The Greek idea of *paideia* is at the conceptual core of the liberationist approach to teaching.

Paideia is the name of a system of education offered in classical Greece and Rome. Its curriculum included gymnastics, rhetoric, philosophy, natural history, music, grammar, mathematics, and geography (note the parallels to Hirst's forms of knowledge). These are the subjects we often think of today when we think of liberal education. Their study makes a person "well rounded," prepares the person generally for life. During the early Christian era, the Greek notion of *paideia* was thought of as *humanitas*—the culture of humankind. In both *paideia* and *humanitas* the focus is on the capacity of human beings to achieve the most noble ends, the highest attainments in knowledge, understanding, and virtue. These notions of excellence in human attainment have persisted in Western thought. They were fundamental notions during the Renaissance and the Enlightenment and continue to be so into the present day. In one form or another, philosophers throughout history have argued for the liberationist approach: not just Plato and Aristotle, but also Erasmus and More, Pascal and Descartes, Hume and Voltaire, Mill and Kant, Whitehead and Dewey.

In the 1980s, a number of books and reports on the state of education in the United States were released. Perhaps the most well known is *A Nation at Risk*, issued by a national commission.[11] Another report that received widespread attention is entitled *The Paideia Proposal*, by Mortimer J. Adler. Decrying the practice of tracking high school students into different preparatory curricula, Adler says:

> Of all the creatures on earth, human beings are the least specialized in anatomical equipment and in instinctive modes of behavior. They are, in consequence, more flexible than other creatures in their ability to adjust to the widest variety of environments and to rapidly changing external circumstances. They are adjustable to every clime and condition on earth and perpetually adjustable to the shock of change.
>
> That is why general, nonspecialized schooling has the quality that most befits human nature. That is why, in terms of practicality and utility, it is better than any other kind of schooling.[12]

Specified knowledge, the goal of the executive approach, is anathema to Adler. Using school time to prepare persons for specific tasks, skills, or jobs is a misuse of school time. The most practical learning is general learning, learning that equips us to realize our adaptability and enables us to perform such tasks as we may confront in a rapidly changing world. General, or liberal, learning is best not only because it capitalizes best on human adaptability and intelligence, but also "because it prepares our children to be good citizens and to lead good human lives."[13]

How would Adler achieve these ends in school settings? His modern answer is not markedly different from the ancient answer. The course of study set forth in *The Paideia Proposal* is a case in point. Adler argues for three major goals: (1) the acquisition of organized knowledge, (2) the development of intellectual skills, which include the skills of learning, and (3) enlarged understanding of ideas and values. Under the first goal, Adler includes three primary areas of subject matter: language, literature, and fine arts; mathematics and natural science; and history, geography, and social studies. Does this sound familiar? We hope so, for these are the forms of knowledge that Hirst contends are critical to the liberationist approach. Adler's second and third goals should also be familiar to you, for you have previously encountered them as part of the discussion of manner in the liberationist approach.

Afterthoughts

The strong emphasis on subject-matter knowledge has troubled many who have looked closely at the liberationist approach. They ask whether it is truly possible or even desirable for all students to study the basic subjects in the way the liberationist argues, especially given the broad range of individual differences in most classrooms. Can all students develop the academic and scholarly minds espoused by the liberationists, or is this approach to teaching really an elitist view of education because its goals can be attained only by a select few? What would be wrong with a more practical approach, aimed at developing the skills and understanding needed for everyday life and work? Indeed, some critics have said that the real question is not the range of differences among students but the range of differences among teachers, that many teachers are simply not able to master and teach the liberationist approach well. Do you agree?

Others argue that the liberationists present too coherent and uniform a picture of knowledge. They contend that most scholars cannot agree on the structure of knowledge in their fields, or if, in fact, there really is any such thing as *the* structure or even *a* structure of knowledge.

Even were some agreement on structure possible, the key concepts and logical forms change over time, making it unwise to try to teach these notions as if they were inherent features of the discipline. The liberationist retort, of course, is that the criticism is essentially defeatist and leaves the teacher with no guidance whatsoever.

The neo-Marxist, critical theorist, or emancipationist also has difficulty with the tradition of liberal education, as it has so often been used as a form of class differentiation and economic oppression. Those with wealth and influence are accorded, by right of birth, a liberal education, which then both enables and entitles them to manage industry, control commerce, and occupy powerful positions in government. Meanwhile the poor and culturally different are afforded only minimal skills, or perhaps a technical education, and as a result become eligible for the less prestigious and less powerful occupations.

The emancipationist would likely agree that this outcome of a liberal education is not somehow tied into the very meaning of liberal education, but is instead the way liberal education is used socially and economically. Even unintentionally it can be and often is an instrument for the privileged classes to maintain their positions of privilege while denying privilege to others. Such denial is not made on the obvious basis of differences in language, race, ethnicity, or gender, but rather on the basis of differences in level and type of educational attainment (as happens when an employment advertisement stipulates that a certain level of schooling is a prerequisite for a position, and the advertisement itself appears in a publication with a circulation that is generally limited to persons who are likely to have such an education). Although this type of class dominance, or cultural reproduction, as the neo-Marxists call it, is not a necessary outgrowth of liberal education, it is most certainly an aspect that requires great vigilance and insight in order to be avoided. We will have more to say on this point in the next chapter.

Yet another important criticism of the liberationist approach is that advanced by Jane Roland Martin. An American philosopher of education, Martin argues that the Hirst-Peters conception of the educated person as someone who has a fully developed mind and has attained a broad cognitive perspective is simply too ivory-tower and narrow a view of what it means to be an educated person. She says:

> The great irony of Hirst's theory of liberal education is that it is neither tolerant nor generous; it conceives of liberal education as the development of mind, restricts the development of mind to the acquisition of knowledge and understanding, and restricts knowledge to true propositions. . . . The received theory's liberally educated person will be taught to

see the world through the lenses of the seven forms of knowledge, if seven there be, but not to act in the world. Nor will that person be encouraged to acquire feelings and emotions. The theory's liberally educated person will be provided with knowledge about others, but will not be taught to care about their welfare, let alone to act kindly toward them. That person will be given some understanding of society, but will not be taught to feel its injustices or even to be concerned over its fate.[14]

Did you get the sense as you read this chapter that the liberationist approach was as heartless as Martin implies? If she is correct, might there be a way of linking the therapist and liberationist approaches, so that the x and the S in $T\phi Sxy$ could both receive emphasis? Or is there a logical and conceptual chasm separating the therapist and the liberationist approaches, just like the one that separates the therapist from the executive? It is time to grapple with these thorny questions, and we will do so in the next chapter. Before you turn to it, you will gain a sharper sense of the liberationist approach by working through the "Freedom and Indoctrination" dispute in chapter 6. You may also want to look at some of the other cases and disputes recommended for this chapter in table 1.

Chapter 5

Reflections on the Three Approaches

Are you ready to decide, or have you already made a decision? Are you confused? Inasmuch as the three approaches appear so different from, even inconsistent with, one another, we tried to pose them in a way that calls for a choice on your part. Let us say you are ready to consider adopting one of the three positions. On what grounds might you choose? There are two simple questions you ought to ponder before deciding: What are the proper standards for an Educated-Person card? What should schools do to qualify persons for this card? Two simple questions? Perhaps not, but trying to answer them may help you considerably in clarifying your choice.

Education and Schooling

For example, let us say that you believe the proper standards for an E-P card are competence in such basic skills as reading, writing, and computation, plus a good liberal education (that is, y = specified knowledge + a liberated mind). Both of these purposes are important to you. But you also believe that the school should be held responsible only for the specified knowledge part of this goal—that is all that can be tested for anyway. Thus even though you believe a person is not fully educated until he or she achieves a liberated mind, you also believe that the school can only be responsible for part of this achievement—the part that involves preparation in the basic skills. Liberation of the mind, you contend, is a lifelong process achieved in the world beyond the school.

If this were your position, you might select the executive approach. It promises to prepare students in the basics in the most effective and efficient manner. The selection seems justified given the distinction you make between education and schooling. Perhaps we should not automatically assume that schools are responsible for everything that makes up a good education. Contributions to education are also made by other institutions like museums, libraries, churches, and performing arts centers, and by parents, peers, the media, and the community. Schooling is just one of the contributors to the E-P card.

Some persons take exception to this view, arguing that education must be a very special activity. It is not something acquired here and there, made up of a little of this experience and a little of that experience. Their view of education is that it should be undertaken to *structure* the experiences we have, not simply be another experience. The philosopher Harry Broudy puts the point rather bluntly:

> When life predicaments can be resolved with common-sense generalizations, one learns by living; when common sense is insufficient, one has to learn by comprehending knowledge discovered and formulated by others. How far do common sense and personal experience go, these days, in thinking about pollution, inflation, the problems of health and peace?[1]

Do you recognize the liberationist approach in these words? Broudy probably would not claim that everything needed for a *first-rate* E-P card should be found in schools, but he would argue that what is found in schools must be quite special—not just another set of ordinary experiences, but the development of disciplined knowledge and understanding that enable students continually to enlarge their horizons, come to grips with the problems and possibilities of life on this planet, and gain a sense of place in the past, present, and future of the human race. It has already been argued (in the last chapter) that the attainment of such laudable goals requires the teacher to explore sophisticated conceptions of knowledge in the traditional subjects and to give careful consideration to the development of manner.

You were cautioned that there are problems with this view. When these noble goals are applied in a system of mass, compulsory schooling, they can have effects just the opposite of the intended goals. Instead of promoting a just, compassionate society, the liberationist approach can and often does end up a great advantage to the highly intelligent and the well-to-do, and a dead-end street for the poor, the racial or ethnic minority, or the less intellectually able from any population of students. The price, it seems, of emphasizing content in the form of highly elaborate conceptions of knowledge is that the teacher leaves behind the very students that many think ought to be ones school really helps (the wealthy and intellectually able will take care of themselves, or so the argument goes).

So far, the choices do not seem terribly attractive. On the one hand we can teach as executives, limiting the content to basic knowledge and skills, while ignoring the lifespace of the learner in our effort to move x efficiently and effectively from source to recipient. Or we can seek to liberate the mind of the learner by exploring knowledge and developing manner in great depth, only to find that the major benefactors of this approach are those who are already economically and academically advantaged. What about the therapist approach; does it represent a way out of the dilemma?

Social and Political Realities

It seems not. Here we must depend on the student to select the content and accept the guidance of the teacher in how to meet and master this content. As a social and political matter, no modern society seems willing to offer choices of this kind to all its students. In these societies, social and political needs usually take precedence over the needs of the individual. For too many key persons—parents, taxpayers, and politicians—the therapist approach appears to be a kind of anarchy. For these persons, school is a place where children must not only learn the basic knowledge and skills needed to function in society, they must learn the game of life—that we cannot do anything we choose to do, that fate and foolishness deal us gentle strokes and hard knocks, and that the world is not peaches and cream.

The obvious personal appeal of the humanistic and existentialist positions does not negate the influence of social and political demands on schools. The existentialist may be correct in asserting that we are free and that the only authentic life we can lead is the one we constantly choose our way toward. It may indeed be true that we are unique and that there are no models to which we must conform, no templates into which we can be squeezed. And it may be that anything worthwhile can only be learned by oneself, never taught by another. Despite these eloquent sentiments on behalf of the individual, we are, as a practical matter, unable to teach in this way in schools as they are. Furthermore, there are sufficient problems of theory and concept with the therapist position to make us wonder whether we should teach that way even if we were permitted to do so.

That last comment may not be fair. As the disputes in chapter 6 show, there are problems of theory and concept with all three approaches, not just the therapist approach. These problems have been compounded by the preceding discussion, where the practical matter of what schools are has been introduced into our deliberations about the three choices. Until this chapter, we have suggested that the choice is yours, to make on such grounds of reason and ethics as you are able to muster. Ah, were life so simple! There are practical matters as well. What does society seek from its schools? What demands will the parents of your students make on you? Do they not have a right to determine the kind of education their children will receive? And then there are some crass, but vital, considerations: How will you be evaluated by the principal and judged by your colleagues? What will determine the increments in your salary? How does one survive as a teacher?

How Shall I Teach?

Now what? Does the position you formulate take account of these realworld exigencies and thus become something of an amalgamation of theory and reality? Or should you ignore these practical matters for now, formulate your position intellectually, then modify it as you gain experience? Or should you just throw in the towel and let life move you along, as the ocean current moves the kelp? These are tough dilemmas, for they raise one of the root questions every human being must confront: How shall I live? Except now the question is a subset of that one: How shall I teach?

We began this chapter by stating that the selection of an approach to teaching would be aided by answering two questions: What are the proper standards for an E-P card? What should the schools do to qualify students for this card? The implication here is that you can answer these questions on your own, without further consideration of the social, economic, and political realities of the context in which you will teach. That implication has now been shown to be incorrect. Any answer that is likely to serve you well must take account of these realities. But there is a critical difference between *taking account of* the realities and allowing them to *determine* what and how you teach.

If you begin with some clear conception of what education is, you have the opportunity to control many of the practical forces that impinge on you, rather than falling victim to these forces. If you have some sense of the purpose of schooling, a sense developed from reflection on theory and ideal, you can shape and direct these realities in ways that support your aspirations for your learners. This activity is not always a struggle of your ideals against the powerful negative forces of the world, for there is much in schools that is already founded on good theory and high ideals. Yet you are not likely to recognize what is there, in either good form or bad, if you cannot recognize where you yourself are.

Thus the first task every teacher must face is to come to some conclusions about the nature and purpose of being an educated person and the place of schooling in achieving this status. These conclusions should be firmly held views, but never set so deeply that they cannot be modified or even uprooted by new experience and insights. The three approaches to teaching we have explored with you here are offered in this spirit: to enable you to begin forming your concept of education and the place of the school within it. We set the approaches up as if they were mutually exclusive, but we did this only as a way to clarify their differences and to illustrate the power and appeal of each of them.

Irreconcilable Differences or Integration?

These are, after all, only *approaches*: different ways of thinking about the same thing, teaching. They provide ways of separating out a myriad of conflicting conceptions so that we can see more clearly what similarities, differences, and problems there are within the jumbled confusion of contemporary educational theory and practice. They do rest on theoretical and ethical ideas that seem logically opposed to one another. Yet we believe that the logical boundaries that separate these positions as scholarly constructions, as ways of thinking about teaching and education, need not be barriers to practical action.

You can, for example, be an executive at times, a therapist at others, a liberationist at still others. In fact, there seem to be situations in teaching that call on you to do just that. There is the fourth-grade student who can barely read or write. You may wonder how he got this far, but he is yours to teach as best you can. Perhaps the best way to help him is to exercise the technical skills of the executive teacher as proficiently as you can. And what of the battered child, who stares through you and barely speaks? Before you can move much of any kind of x to that child, you must help her deal with a world that has overwhelmed her. The learners who are fully up to speed may profit from the liberationist approach, exploring knowledge and manner as deeply as their abilities permit.

Did that last sentence disturb you? It was a "ringer." If you use the liberationist approach only for learners already "fully up to speed," you may exacerbate the conditions of inequality in schools. Then only the more able learners would receive the advanced content and instruction, and that would place the less able learners at an increasing disadvantage. There is a clear danger to education if these approaches are integrated in certain ways. If you think of these approaches as options to be selected for different learners or situations, you run the risk of condemning students to preestablished categories for instruction. This sometimes happens in the case of ability groups and in the tracking that occurs in secondary schools. When grouped in these ways, learners can become trapped in their assigned categories. The incorrigible learners are taught by therapists and allowed to self-select what they will learn (not because we believe that is the right and proper way to educate, but because we have no luck getting them to do anything else); the average learners are instructed by teacher-executives so that they acquire the so-called basic competencies; and the advanced learners are encouraged to delve deeply into the broad range of human knowledge. And thus the gap among the incorrigible, the average, and the academically able grows greater and greater. A situation of this type justifies the accusations of the emancipationists, for this is precisely what they mean by the oppressive character of schooling and its capacity to reproduce the culture rather than to renew and recreate it.

From a practical standpoint, some of this differentiation is an inevitable consequence of good instruction, no matter what approach is used. That is, those who are ready and able to gain from school will do so more quickly and more completely than those who are less ready. The absolutely critical consideration is to avoid predetermining who will gain, and at what rates, by teaching one group of children according to an approach that keeps them from growing in ways that another group is growing from their exposure to a different approach.

Endthoughts

You have probably guessed where we are leading you. The normative nature of teaching demands a commitment to worthy educational values, and each of these three approaches contains something of value. If you are committed to having your students gain to the fullest extent possible from their experiences of schooling, we believe you must try to put these three approaches together somehow while avoiding the pitfalls of doing so. We also believe that this task is not so impossible in practice as the theoretical differences in each approach suggest. It is not easy either.

Integration will require a sensitivity to factors in concrete situations that call for a delicate balancing of your values, purposes, and actions. There are no easy recipes and you may not always succeed. Of course, you may decide, for good reasons, that the advantages of adopting one approach far exceed the disadvantages of attempting integration. Your choice of a normative view of teaching should rest on your own best judgment. This is why we have offered a consideration of the negative as well as the positive features of each approach in this book. The choice is yours. In the end, if our position is tempting, you will have to decide whether integration is worth trying. We can only offer some observations that have helped us in our own teaching to try to honor these different points of view.

In our view, all three approaches to teaching are critically important to being a good teacher. However, only the liberationist position provides a broad theoretical foundation for the general activity of teaching. The liberationist approach has the advantage of age (it has been "under development" since the time of Socrates) as well as completeness (no other approach has so fully expressed a view of rational and moral conduct in relation to the nature of education). For us, this approach, more than the other two, specifies what it means to qualify for the Educated-Person card. As such, it serves as bedrock for guiding our work as teachers.[2]

However, as already noted, the liberationist approach contains inherent dangers. In many of the versions of its advocates, it is insensitive to human differences and too rigidly prescribed. Aside from these inherent weaknesses, it has a major structural disadvantage. It is readily adaptable as an instrument for maintaining class privilege and for engendering destructive differentiations based on wealth, power, cultural background, race, and gender. The emancipationists have done a great service in pointing out the downside of liberal education, but they have not offered an educational alternative anywhere near as profound and complete as what they propose to replace. Indeed, in a way, one might see them struggling to do liberal education right, without the harmful side effects that they have so thoughtfully documented.

If it were possible to educate everyone in discrete, nurturing enclaves, such as warm, caring nuclear families united in small, cohesive communities, not only might the liberationist approach serve as the bedrock for teaching, it might also be a sufficient guide for success as a teacher. But we are not living in a time of nurturing enclaves of committed adults. Shifts in demography and social structure have brought increasing demands on schools to accomplish for most children and youth what used to be accomplished by parents, churches, and communities in the past. The executive and therapist approaches are needed for successful teaching in systems of schooling as they now exist. Both offer perspectives and methods that permit teachers to practice effectively and humanely in the complex, highly differentiated classrooms of today.

Returning to the formula $T\phi Sxy$, the executive and therapist approaches offer a great deal to the definition of ϕ, although not very much to the definition of y (save that the therapist notion of authenticity is, we believe, an important contribution to the purposes of education). The liberationist approach, in contrast, provides a great deal of definition to y, and while it also contributes to the content of ϕ in terms of "manner," much of this must be inferred from theoretical views about the nature of mind, knowledge, virtue, and human action.

The executive approach demands technical skill as a teacher. This skill need not be employed solely to move some highly specified x from source to recipient, although it often gets articulated that way because highly structured curriculum materials and standardized testing requirements so frequently accompany calls for the executive approach. However, you can learn useful techniques, develop effective pedagogical skills, and be accountable for proficient instruction without forfeiting the opportunity to explore content areas in depth, to emphasize the structure and interrelatedness of knowledge, and to engage in a manner intended to nurture the moral and intellectual virtues.

Much the same may be said of the therapist approach. Becoming connected to the personal lives of children does not mean one must abandon a serious commitment to their academic development. Indeed, with many of today's schoolchildren, one cannot be seriously committed to their academic development without in some ways engaging in their lives as children in settings other than the school. From the therapist perspective, one's aim is far more than getting learners to acquire knowledge and skill. It is also enabling and empowering them to use, interpret, and extend what is learned in ways that advance their own sense of identity and meaningfulness. For the therapist, the wisdom of humankind cannot become wisdom for learners unless they make it their own, working it through by and for themselves.

Thus we believe that while there may be contradictions among these approaches at the level of concept or theory, there need be no such opposition at the level of practice. If you have a strong and well-articulated sense of what an educated person should be, then you will be ready to make the most important decision any teacher can make. No approach to teaching should be embraced solely because it fits well with the temper of the times, or because it works in your classroom, or because the school board or the principal promulgated it. These are weak and insufficient grounds for the crucial choice of how to teach.

So, in the end, if you would try to integrate your approach to teaching you must seek to free not just the mind but the heart and the spirit as well. To do this, you may have to compromise the theoretical purity of the three approaches and dig deeply into what humankind thinks it knows and into yourself to learn what the known means to you and how you will live. And you must do this *for* your learners, *before* your learners, where they can see the manner of an educated person and choose to model themselves after you. Then you truly will have become a teacher.

Chapter 6

Reflections for the Third Time

Not long after the publication of the revised and expanded second edition of this book, we began talking about how the book might be improved. These conversations were delightful but disjointed explorations among two old friends, until the time drew near to actually begin work on a third edition. Once that time was upon us, we knew we had to become more focused in our endeavors. There were new research studies to attend to, new theories to incorporate, plus the wisdom gained from using the second edition in teacher education courses (for which we thank our students, and our faculty colleagues who used the book and wrote to us about their experiences with it).

Our first concern was with the three categories: Executive, Therapist, Liberationist. We wondered if they were still viable. If not, how should they be changed? We also wondered whether there were newer approaches than those we discussed in the first and second editions, and if so, if they were well enough developed for inclusion in this book. After considerable discussion, we decided to leave the heart of the book unchanged, adding only this new chapter. The reason we did so is that the three approaches have not changed so significantly that we would be required to discard them in favor of other approaches. However, there has been some evolution in at least two of the approaches. We decided that the best way to report on this evolution was to leave the main part of the book unchanged while adding this chapter.

The approaches are not the only thing that has evolved. Our thinking about the approaches has also changed. Again, we faced the decision whether to modify the extant approaches to reflect the shifts in our own thinking, or leave the original approaches alone, adding material that would indicate the changes that we made in our thinking. By this time, you know that we took the latter course. Thus this chapter does two things: It reports on new developments affecting the three approaches, and it describes our own changes of mind as we thought again about these approaches.

Although the status of the three approaches was our first concern in deciding how to undertake the third edition, we had another major concern. Our second concern pertained to the way we framed the argument of the book, particularly our effort to press you, the reader, to keep the three approaches distinct from one another. Quite a few of you expressed annoyance at our insisting that you choose one approach over the others, then asserting in chapter 5 that although the three approaches are incompatible in theory they might get along fine with one another in practice. Some of you disliked the feeling of our directing you to a position we had no intention of retaining later in the book. Others chastised us for "copping out" by taking such a strong stance against compatibility, then concluding the book with some wishy-washy, not-so-well-developed ideas about how the approaches might hospitably take up residence in the same teacher.

We have had nearly 15 years to think about this matter (the first edition was published in 1986), and we are still puzzling over its resolution. Part of what makes this issue so complicated is our realization that we were undervaluing the executive and therapist positions in relation to the liberationist position. We tried to be careful about not showing our biases, at least not until chapter 5, but we did not do so well on this score (on our view of the matter). The executive and therapist approaches, especially as you will encounter them in just a moment, have more integrity and power than we realized. As such, the general worth of the three approaches is better balanced than we thought when preparing the first and second editions.

So what, you ask. What does this balance have to do with whether or not you can practice two or even three approaches serially or simultaneously? Glad you asked (you did, didn't you?). The better these approaches are framed, that is, the more integrity and power each has, the more they appear mutually incompatible. Surprised? Well, let's see what you think of our argument.

Are the Three Approaches Compatible?

Not long ago, Kieran Egan, a first rate educational thinker at Simon Fraser University in British Columbia, wrote a book entitled, *The Educated Mind: How Cognitive Tools Shape Our Understanding.*[1] In the opening argument of this book, Egan contends that so many of the difficulties we encounter with schooling are the result of "a fundamentally incoherent conception of education" (p. 2). As you read his summary of this conception of education, keep the three approaches in mind.

> Educational theorizing is generally dreary because we have only three significant educational ideas: that we must shape the young to the current norms and conventions of adult society, that we must teach them the knowledge that will ensure their thinking conforms with what is real and true about the world, and that we must encourage the development of each student's individual potential. (p. 3)

Egan then gives us the good news and the bad news (literally): "The good news, I suppose, is that there are indeed only three ideas to grasp. The bad news is that the three ideas are mutually incompatible" (p. 3). As you may have noted, Egan's views bear quite dramatically on the three approaches. The parallels are not exact, but close enough to make it worthwhile to attend carefully to the argument Egan is making about how the three grand aims of education are mutually incompatible.

The first major idea is that the purpose of education is to "shape the young to the current norms and conventions of adult society." We trust that evoked a remembrance of the executive approach, for that is the major justification of this approach (recall that in this approach, the teacher's task is to convey the content, *x*, to *S*, the student, the point of which is to ready the young for productive places in adult society). As we presented the executive approach in chapter 2, it was more about method than about aim, although you may recall that we remarked how well suited executive methods were to conventional social aims for schools (we have more to say about that below). Egan sees a serious incompatibility between socialization and the second idea, cultivating the intellectual capacities of the young. This second idea, which he attributes to Plato, is akin to the liberationist approach. It is incompatible with socialization because the one fosters compliance and conformity while the other fosters skepticism and autonomy. Athens compelled Socrates, Plato's teacher, to drink hemlock because he was corrupting the morals of youth, encouraging them to question, to think for themselves. In other words, Athens sought socialization as the aim, while Socrates and Plato would sacrifice the social good for the higher good of knowledge and truth.

Egan's third idea, the development of each student's potential, is attributed to Rousseau, whose classic work, *Émile*, describes the rearing of a child in the most pristine, natural circumstances possible, to the end of having the child's own talents and capacities emerge without the constraining effects of any "system" of schooling. This third idea is, of course, akin to the therapist approach to teaching. Egan does not need to stretch a point to show its incompatibility to socialization and true knowledge as the other two aims. If one is engaged in socialization, then one is imposing norms, customs, and conduct on the learner, all highly inconsistent with the free and unfettered unfolding of the natural child. If one is engaged in the cultivation of true knowledge, one is also imposing, but this time the imposition is not with customs and conduct, but with analytical ways of thinking and with the concepts, methods, and theories of the various branches of human knowledge.

When speaking of how these ideas work out in classrooms, Egan comments on what happens when, for example, teachers favoring Plato butt heads with teachers inclined towards Rousseau:

The former argue for a more structured curriculum, logically sequenced, and including the canonical knowledge of Western "high" culture; the latter argue for activities that encourage students to explore the world around them and, in as far as they are willing to prespecify curriculum content, they propose knowledge relevant to students' present and likely future experience. (p. 23)

After describing several of these tensions, Egan makes a remark that smacks of innumerable conversations we have had with our students:

Clearly few teachers adhere to one position to the exclusion of others; most teachers try to balance all of them in practice. So, for example, even Rousseau-inclined teachers tend to acknowledge the importance of the canonical content of the Plato-influenced curriculum; their compromise between incompatibles means that they feel it is important to "expose" students to the "high culture" curriculum content but they feel no imperative to persist with it for students who do not take to it. That is, each idea is allowed enough scope to undercut the other. (p. 23)

What does Egan do about these problems? He proposes a new theory, one that discards the three grand, but conflicting, aims of education. In their place, he proposes a conception of how to foster the development of children that integrates their interests with those of the larger society. This new theory is not of immediate interest here (we recommend the book to you), although it carries a fascinating implication for the three approaches. All three are essential, although which is primary while the others are secondary would vary with the type of understanding the educator is seeking to foster in the learner. Could it be that so many of our readers have been right all along? Can all three approaches be practiced without conflict or incompatibility, and are all three jointly important to the good education of the learner? We still want to say, it depends . . . .

Egad, you say, will these guys never give up? What is it going to take to straighten them out? Before we get too far along in explaining why we are so stubborn, we think it would be a good idea to take a fresh look at each of the three approaches. We try to bring them up-to-date by looking at what has happened with each since the last edition of the book, and pondering what this new information means for the general character of that approach. We find this endeavor fascinating, turning over the older ideas in light of new thinking. We hope we engage in this activity in a way that permits you to observe how some fairly important educational ideas have evolved in less than a decade.

Revisiting the Executive Approach

The executive approach is still very much with us. Although there has been a somewhat diminished emphasis on studying the technical aspects of teaching (as occurred during the 1970s and 1980s), educational policy initiatives in the United States strongly favor an executive approach to teaching. Recall that in this approach, there is a marked emphasis on student learning outcomes based on fixed conceptions of what students should know and be able to do. These outcomes are precisely what state and federal educational policy are promoting as the twentieth century comes to an end.

State after state has adopted standardized achievement tests, and many policy makers have advocated for tests of this kind as a key part of the agenda for educational reform in the 21st century. The results of these tests are published, typically on a school by school basis, annually in home town newspapers across the United States. School boards, business leaders, real estate agents, and parents are among those who take a great deal of interest in the results of such tests. As such, there is enormous pressure on teachers to produce higher levels of attainment on the part of their students. This pressure provides great inducement to take the executive approach seriously, for this is the approach that is most concerned with acquiring knowledge, skill, and dispositions valued by the larger society.

The executive approach can indeed provide a powerful way to achieve such goals. The problem is how the teacher conceives of executive teaching. If, as we stated in chapter 2, the desired outcome is simply the acquisition of specified knowledge, then the attainments of the students are likely to be at a fairly low level. If, on the other hand, we focused on a more robust concept, say competence, as the outcome (changing the value of y in $T\phi Sxy$ from "acquiring specified knowledge" to "becoming competent as a citizen, parent, and worker"), then the executive approach becomes a more sophisticated approach to teaching than we implied in previous editions. On this revised account of the executive approach, the teacher is more than a manager, taking on such additional roles as leader, guide, coach, and interpreter of difficult subject matter. Of course he or she may also retain the style of task master, "drill sergeant," or other, less dramatic, "no nonsense, let's get down to business" techniques.

As we reflect on the executive approach, competence does indeed appear to be its primary end-in-view. Moreover, this end is typically attained through a process of conveyance or transmission. On this account, the teacher is clear about the knowledge and skill to be acquired for competence in the multiple roles of, say, citizen, worker, and parent, and goes about the tasks of conveying this knowledge and skill in a business-like, professional manner. Given this conception of teaching, it seems quite reasonable to appraise the results with end-of-year tests pegged to a standard curriculum specifying what every child should know and be able to do. This view of teaching, as noted earlier, is held by many persons engaged in the promulgation of educational policy at state and federal levels. The presumption of these policy makers and educational reformers is that our youth need to learn certain things if they are to become capable, competent citizens and workers in a globally competitive society. They also believe that once we identify the essential skills and necessary knowledge for effectively performing multiple adult roles and tasks, we can specify a curriculum detailing this knowledge and these skills, then call upon teachers to effectively teach it to students.

Although there are close links between contemporary educational policy initiatives and the executive approach to teaching, it is very important to keep the two distinct. The executive approach should not to be judged better or worse because it seems to be favored by current policy initiatives. It is more than capable of standing alone, judged on its merits as one of the primary approaches to teaching. As seen from the vantage point of late 1998, it is a worthy contender for a teacher's consideration, particularly in those cases where the principal outcome sought is competence and the prevailing view of knowledge and skill is that they can be specified ahead of actual instruction and faithfully conveyed from their repositories to the minds and bodies of learners.

That last sentence exposes a possible fly in the ointment. The analogy of knowledge and skill being conveyed or transmitted, as if they were freight hauled from texts and worksheets to the heads of students, is under heavy attack by advocates for a school of thought known as *constructivism*. Constructivists argue that the meaning ideas or experiences have for a learner is not pre-packaged with the idea or the experience, but is constructed by the learner in the course of engaging the idea or having the experience. This theory of how we learn has a number of antecedents, ranging from the Swiss psychologist and philosopher, Jean Piaget, and the Russian psychologist, Lev Vygotsky, to a number of contemporary cognitive psychologists, particularly those specializing in a sub-field known as situated cognition.[2]

Constructivism represents a challenge to the executive approach because it denies the possibility of conveying knowledge and skill intact. Instead, knowledge and skill are believed to be "taken on" by learners, who frame the meaning of this knowledge and skill on the basis of their prior knowledge and skill, as well as their personal biographies (meaning, for example, that a learner reared in poverty is likely to interpret many ideas and experiences differently from a learner reared in affluence). Constructivist teachers typically assign a high value to discussion and dialogue in their classrooms, for it is through such conversational interactions that learners gain the opportunity to make explicit the meaning they are giving to new experiences, as well as to observe and ponder the meaning given to these experiences by classmates. In addition, constructivist teachers are wary of right answers; an insistence on a particular answer would, in many cases, deny learners the opportunity to explore the meaning an idea has for them. Given these facets of constructivist teaching, it is an obvious inference that constructivist teachers are generally very student-centered.

Does being student-centered, having lots of dialogue during class time, and avoiding a right-answer approach to knowledge mean that a person who embraces a constructivist theory of learning cannot adopt an executive approach to teaching? For the many scholars currently debating the topic of constructivism, this is a most interesting question. The no-nonsense, competency-oriented, specified curriculum features of the executive approach appear to place it in opposition to constructivist conceptions of how to teach. We, on the other hand, are not so certain. While there is certainly a stronger kinship between constructivism and the therapist and emancipatory approaches to teaching, we believe that a person could be an executive and a constructivist at the same time—although we confess we are stretching the point.[3]

Before we explore why constructivism has a tighter connection to the therapist and emancipatory approaches, it may be helpful to summarize this discussion of the executive approach. The teaching techniques described in chapter 2 have changed little since the second edition. Rather, our sense of the purpose of these techniques has altered, and as a result, this approach takes on greater value and importance than we accorded it in previous editions. Competence, in the best sense of the term, is certainly a worthy aim of education, a noble y in the expression $T\phi Sxy$. It is the view of knowledge, and therefore of curriculum and subject matter content (the x in $T\phi Sxy$), that is the currently contested feature of the executive approach. The dispute is whether knowledge and skill can be pre-specified for all learners, so that they will acquire this knowledge and skill in some established sequence, with fairly uniform outcomes. You may recall that the therapist found this conception of knowledge ignored the interests and needs of different learners, while the liberationist argued it inhibited efforts to foster the moral and intellectual virtues so vital to human flourishing. To these concerns we can now add the concern of the constructivists, who find the views of knowledge implicit in the executive approach counter to the constructivist conception of how children learn. Does the executive teacher revise her account of knowledge, in order to accommodate these criticisms, or would that so alter the nature of the executive approach as to be a wrong-headed move? Let's leave this question for a bit, returning to it at the conclusion of this chapter.

Revisiting the Therapist Approach

Of the three approaches described in this book, the therapist approach proved the most difficult for us to describe adequately in the first two editions. Perhaps we should not be too surprised by the challenge of representing the therapist position, since it is a part of the defining characteristics of this approach to resist specificity and categorization (for all the reasons we set forth in chapter 3). Yet even the name *therapist* bothered us. We tried to be very clear that this approach was pertinent to all learners, not simply those with special needs. However the very title, "The Therapist Approach," carries the implication that it is intended for learners who have problems, as we usually think of contacting a therapist only when things have gone awry and we are in need of help. We simply could not think of a better name to give to teaching intended primarily to foster the individual development of the whole child, for the purpose of assisting that child in becoming not so much an informed citizen or a competent worker, as in the case of the executive approach, but rather a fulfilled, self-actualized human being.

Now, thanks in large part to more recent scholarship in this area, we think we have a better idea of how to describe this approach to teaching. Indeed, if we were to rewrite the entire book, this approach is the only one we would rename. We would call it "The Fostering Approach." This expression probably sounds odd to you, as it initially did to us, as this particular use of the term *foster* is not very common. However, consider these definitions from *The American Heritage Dictionary* (Third Edition): "1. To bring up; nurture. 2. To promote the growth and development of; cultivate. 3. To nurse; cherish." In its adjectival form, the term "foster" is defined as providing parental care and nurture to children not related through legal or blood ties, as in the example of foster parents. These definitions provide a much better description of what we intended in the first two editions. They also describe more accurately the teachers we observe who exhibit the characteristics of the approach we previously called "therapist."

A bit of caution is in order. The correct expression here is "fostering teacher," not "foster teacher" (a foster teacher sounds too much like a variety of substitute teacher; that is, someone who takes the place of the real or legally legitimate teacher). A fostering teacher is committed to the ends-in-view we described in chapter 3: The personal development of the whole child, building confidence and self-esteem, the cultivation of the authentic self, the promotion of self-actualization. However, more recent scholarship indicates that these ends may not be what truly defines the fostering approach to teaching.

The work of Lawrence Blum, Carol Gilligan, and Nel Noddings on an ethic of care, and of Donna Kerr on what nurture requires of all persons, particularly in democratic settings, is critical to our conception of the fostering approach to teaching.[4] In addition to these scholars, Jane Roland Martin's work on the concept of the "schoolhome," Annette Baier's essays on trust, and John Goodlad's reflections on pedagogical nurturing all play a part in framing the concept of a fostering approach.[5] This scholarship is marked by two essential beliefs: (1) that how human beings are connected to one another in relationships is fundamental to how these human beings fare in life, and (2) that there is a profound moral case to be made for human relationships characterized by care, nurture, trust, and love (each of these terms picks out different forms of human relationship, and varies by the theorist discussing them, but all point to a fairly uniform set of ideas in the context of exploring what is involved in a fostering approach to teaching).

The fostering teacher is concerned with the nature and quality of the relationship between him- or herself and the students. Thus in the expression $T\phi Sxy$, we would mark the focus of the fostering approach as $T+S$, not just S as we did in the therapist approach. The fostering approach is marked less by the outcome of the relationship (such as self-actualization), as was the case in the therapist approach, and more by the nature of the relationship. In so stating, we do not mean to imply that outcomes are not important in fostering, only that they are defined in terms of the nature and quality of the relationship rather than in terms of some non-relational good. For example, Donna Kerr places a high value on democratic character as an outcome of education, but argues that such character cannot be well formed in the absence of relationships of nurture, relationships where persons show regard for and interest in one another on the grounds of their humanness alone.[6]

Recasting the therapist approach as the fostering approach has an impact on the two of us not unlike what happened when we changed the goal of the executive approach to competence: It becomes a stronger approach, a vigorous alternative to the executive and liberationist approaches. What distinguishes this approach from the executive and the liberationist is what the teacher values most about the work of teaching. It is not the formation of competent citizens and workers, as in the executive approach—although no advocate for the fostering approach we know would deny the importance of competent citizens and workers.

It is not the cultivation of rational, critical, reflective thinkers and agents who are deeply acquainted with the accumulated wisdom of civilization, as in the liberationist approach—although again we know of no proponents of fostering who would impugn these liberationist goals. What the advocate for fostering contends is that the worthy ends of the executive and the liberationist are not likely to be achieved in any morally satisfactory way in the absence of relationships of a certain kind between teacher and learner. These relationships are founded on care, trust, concern, and nurture.

In contrast to some lingering implications of the therapist approach described in chapter 3, it is important to make clear here that the fostering approach does not necessarily involve "open" classrooms, or high levels of student freedom and choice, nor is the fostering teacher any less likely to emphasize subject matter content than the executive or liberationist teacher. While it may be the case that emphasis on relationship leads to more open classrooms, with greater degrees of choice, fostering teachers may also exercise care for their students by limiting their choices and confining the options available to them. Moreover, fostering teachers may involve their students in extensive and profound explorations of subject matter. What distinguishes them from executives and liberationists in this activity is that ends to be attained by such explorations seldom, if ever, justify abandoning the primacy of the relational bond between teacher and student.

We find ourselves far more comfortable with the concept of fostering than we did with that of therapist. Recent ethical studies in philosophy and the remarkable contributions of feminist scholars in the social sciences and humanities offer a better grounding for this approach than was provided by the existentialists and humanistic psychologists of mid-century (there is a historical progression here, however). Fortunately the surgery required in the case of the liberationists is not so extensive, but some repair is definitely in order.

Revisiting the Liberationist Approach

As in the case for the executive approach, we may have changed more than the approach itself has changed. It is not that no changes have occurred to the liberationist approach, for they have. It is rather that we set up the liberationist approach in a way that tilted it too far to the classical view of liberation, not the critical view (which we called the emancipatory view in chapter 4, treating it as a variant of the main, liberationist approach). Sufficient scholarship has emerged in support of the emancipationist view that we believe it deserves stand-alone recognition. Indeed, that may have been the proper stance in the second edition, where it unfortunately receives the kind of consideration that may lead a reader to regard it as a kind of second cousin to liberation.

The interesting twist here is that the liberationist and emancipationist share many of the same ends (the y in $T\phi Sxy$), but believe that getting there calls for thinking about knowledge (x) in a different way as well as a different method for teaching this knowledge (ϕ). Because both liberationist and emancipationist share similar ends, we believe that clarity and coherence would be improved by referring to a single approach, the liberationist, with alternative views about how the aims of this approach are to be obtained. The classical liberationist is just what we described in chapter 4 as the liberationist. The critical liberationist is what we previously called the emancipationist. For ease of reference, and a wee bit of fun, we sometimes refer to the classical liberationists as "classlibs," and to the critical liberationists as "critlibs."

Our description of the classlibs in chapter 4 smacks a bit too much of resting on the traditional forms of knowledge (the academic disciplines, sometimes also referred to as "The Western Canon"). On hindsight, we believe that classical liberation may have more to do with the initiation of the learner into ways of knowing in a field rather than just acquiring the knowledge and understanding of the traditional disciplines.[7] It is not just sophisticated knowledge that the classical liberationist teacher has and wants to "convey" to the learner. The classlib is an "insider," a person who really knows his or her field; i.e., who knows what it takes to be a participant in the generation and use of a certain kind of knowledge. He or she is a member of a community of knowers. Having been inducted into this community through years of study and perhaps even apprenticeship, the teacher is at least a journeyman, if not a master of the field (by "field," we mean to include such areas of study as health, physical education, and vocational education as well as the more traditional fields, such as mathematics, history, and physics). The aim of the teacher as initiator is to bring the student into a field as a participant, as a member of an intellectual and moral community. Being a community, it requires values and virtues to govern the proper behavior of its members, as well as a common language and shared ways of doing and thinking. Each field has a history, a set of traditions, exemplars of good work, a group of heroes, and perhaps villains, too. Initiation is an introduction to, a beginning to understand, what a field is about. It is an experience *in* the field, not just information *about* the field.

Classical liberation is probably the finest attainment of this form of initiation, but it can become, as we saw in chapter 4, another form of transmission or conveyor education. To avoid this consequence, it is vital for teachers of all subjects to grasp the nature of their subject as a field of inquiry, as a body of knowledge and set of methods, as a way of coming to understand some things a bit better from the vantage point of one's knowledge community. On this view, teachers from many different fields, not just the standard academic disciplines, can be classical liberationists. However, to claim membership here, a teacher must truly have a deep understanding of his or her field, to be a master of this field in the best sense of the term.

This expansion of our understanding of classical liberation contrasts with the need to recast rather completely the discussion of emancipation in chapter 4. The emancipationists (who we now call critical liberationists, or critlibs) contend that human reason, knowledge, and values do not come packaged nearly so neatly as the classical liberationist would have us believe. These products of the human mind, argue the critlibs, are deeply influenced by wealth, power, and prestige. To understand this point, consider our views of what constitutes good literature, art, or music. Is opera superior to rap because of some inherent feature of music, wherein we can objectively determine that, for example, Wagner's *Flying Dutchman* is musically superior to Puff Daddy's *No Way Out*? There are certainly those who would so argue, including a broad spectrum of classlibs. However, look carefully at who is making this argument; look at their cultural backgrounds and their social class. What is often observed is that persons of privilege, who are members of the dominant or majority culture, are the ones arguing for the superiority of Wagner over Puff Daddy.

When persons of status and privilege who are members of the dominant culture argue in this way, they do two things according to the critical liberationists. First, they set the standards for what is true, good, and right, establishing these standards not only for themselves, but for everyone whose lives are affected by the dominant or majority group. Second, they often directly or by implication demean or impugn alternative forms, the forms typically developed by persons who lack power and privilege, or who are members of subordinate or minority cultures. The critlibs claim that it is these social and economic mechanisms that lead us to value Wagner's opera over Puff Daddy's rap. From their point of view, the presumed superiority is not the result of some inherent feature of the music itself, or of universal, objective standards for aesthetic goodness. Instead, they believe that this is how the dominant group functions relative to subordinate groups, as the dominant group seeks to preserve itself and its power and privilege.

Regardless of your reaction to this particular example, let us assume that the the arguments of the critical liberationists hold sufficient merit to be taken seriously as an approach to teaching. What would such an approach look like? Until recently the question of what kind of teaching is called for in critical liberation has been difficult to answer, for the critical liberationists expended so much of their energy denouncing the consequences of traditional schooling, rather than formulating teaching practices congruent with their own theories.[8] In the last several years, however, work has emerged that shows us how teaching looks when it is grounded in critical perspectives. Among the more helpful efforts in this regard is Ira Shor's *Empowering Education.*[9]

For Shor, critical teaching involves a number of central factors. Because many of these factors are also found in the work of others, such as Patricia Hinchey and Joan Wink,[10] they are worthy of our attention here. As you might expect, the first, and perhaps most central, feature of critical liberation is: Attend to the students, each and all. In doing so, the teacher does not emphasize what she or the society wants the student to become, as the executive teacher might, nor does she nurture each individual's unique potential as the fostering teacher might. Instead the critlib teacher attends to how students see and locate themselves in the world, and how their vision of social reality conditions what they want to become. Because the student's desire to become something is most likely influenced by the dominant traditions and values in that student's life, a central task of critical teaching is to assist the student in seeing how his or her life is constructed by such things as the norms, traditions, rules, and values of the dominant group in his or her society.

Sometimes called conscientization (following Paulo Freire, who first explicated the term),[11] this process of assisting students to gain insight into how their social world works to shape them is a vital part of critical liberation, for coming to understand what others are trying to make us into or get us to do is an important step in achieving our own liberation. Conscientization requires the teacher to avoid accepting matters as they appear, and instead frame the objects of study as problems for students to deal with in the unmasking of social categories. For example, the innocent question, "What do you want to be when you grow up?" cannot be taken simply on its face," whereby the educator assists the student in becoming what he wishes to become. The critical liberationist makes this simple query problematic by asking what leads the student to seek that occupation; whether there is a connection between that occupation and the student's sense of his own abilities and opportunities; whether students of similar race, gender, or physical feature also select this occupation; whether there are other occupations that the student might consider but feels ineligible to select.

As you might have inferred from that last, long sentence, the critical liberationist would not be satisfied with some ordinary career education or job training program as an aid to assisting the student in selecting a career. She would want the students to inquire into why certain occupations are discussed in certain neighborhoods, or among certain social strata, or among students whose families have a certain level of income. She would want to encourage her students to ponder such considerations, and she would encourage them to study carefully why matters are as they appear to be and what can be done about them. She would want them to free themselves from unconsciously held restraints to their freedom of choice. It is not enough, however, for the student to grasp the problematic nature of a situation or experience; the student must seek a resolution to the problem. The search for a resolution involves not only study and reflection, but also action.

Action, or *praxis*, as it is often called by the critlibs, is another very important part of critical teaching. Students are called upon not only to think and to learn, but to do. This doing may not always involve a significant, formal act (such as a going against the grain of "official" advice, joining a protest rally, promoting a ballot initiative, or writing letters to the editor), but might be so simple as holding oneself accountable to never again act in certain ways which unconsciously deny one's own or another's freedom to speak or choose, or their desire to be recognized and understood.

If you return to chapter 4, reading again the description of the liberationists and emancipationists, you will, we think, note some rather substantial differences. The classlibs value the accumulated wisdom and understanding of the human race, and perceive formal education as the place to acquire and appreciate this treasure of civilization. One of the most articulate spokespersons for liberal learning, Michael Oakeshott, called this store of knowledge and understanding a great human conversation, "an endless unrehearsed intellectual adventure in which, in imagination, we enter into a variety of modes of understanding the world and ourselves and are not disconcerted by the differences or dismayed by the inconclusiveness of it all."[12]

Classlibs want learners to acquire this accumulated knowledge and under-standing so that they can join into the human conversation. The critlibs re-spond that the conversation is controlled by those with wealth and power, and that it should not be one conversation, but many. The classlibs believe that there must be such things as grounds for argument, rules of logic, and evidence for knowledge, while the critlibs question whose rules, whose grounds, whose evidence. It would be an error to presume, however, that the critlibs believe that the classlib knowledge is wrong, or irrelevant. Critlibs may place a high value on classlib knowledge, but only if it is freely and con-sciously accessible to all, if it is not used as a tool for dominion or oppres-sion, and if it is understood that our situated lives may require us to interpret knowledge differently from what orthodoxy appears to require.

We hope we have offered a better perspective on critical liberation than our discussion of the emancipatory perspective in chapter 4. We cannot leave the topic just yet, though. The previous example comparing Richard Wagner and Puff Daddy still has us thinking. Would critical liberation theory require that we value Puff Daddy, or any other artistic talent, equally with Wagner? The answer is not entirely clear, as it depends on how radical or postmodern the critical theorist happens to be. Most critical liberationists would permit a general determination that some things, achievements, or events may prop-erly be assigned a higher value relative to other things. However, the critical liberationist would call on us to take great care not to assign this value based solely on occupying a position of privilege or power. Thus, Wagner may en-dure from century to century, and Puff Daddy may not. That one survives and the other does not may be the result of superior musical attainment. Or it may be that one class of persons insists on embracing Wagner as a means of excluding another class. The critical liberationist would want us to be very careful about why this happens, and whether it is happening in a way that silences some voices while privileging others.

These thoughts on how the classical and critical liberationists might re-spond to questions about the value of cultural artifacts provide an occasion to raise another important consideration, that of multiculturalism. Our first instinct was to include this discussion under the liberationist heading, since it is so much a part of the critlib discourse. However, it would be an injustice to the executive and fostering approaches to imply that the liberationist has a corner on multicultural sensitivity or scholarship. We therefore decided to treat the topic in a separate section, to which we now turn.

The Multicultural Aspects of Approaches to Teaching

Multiculturalism is both a complex term and a contested idea in contempo-rary American society. Yet few ideas hold as much significance for education.

If we were to collect the key words about education in one place, the list would surely include such words as democracy, knowledge, critical awareness, competence, authenticity, and virtuousness. In these times, it is also likely to include multicultural understanding. Yet the fact that multiculturalism has become so prominent a term in the educational domain does not mean that we are clear about its definition or its application. The concept is currently subject to intense debate, as lawsuits are filed against affirmative action policies and referenda are completed or underway seeking an end to many forms of bilingual education. These contemporary disputes serve as indicators of how contested is the ground upon which multiculturalism rests.

There can be little doubt that some of the disputes over the nature and purpose of multiculturalism are inspired by ignorance or prejudice (or both). However one may also find bewilderment or frustration with multiculturalism expressed by persons who appear reasonably free of racial or ethnic bias. Among the more thought-provoking concerns one hears about multiculturalism is how to balance regard for difference (often known as pluralism or diversity) with a sense of what is common to a nation, its people, and its government. Many political theorists believe that in democracies such as that practiced in the United States, holding things in common across all the people is essential to sustain a healthy, fully functioning democracy. Among the features generally believed necessary to be held in common are language, heroic stories, traditions, core values, and historical memory; all of these are associated with a range of duties and obligations to one's fellow citizens and one's government. For some persons, multiculturalism threatens this commonness, replacing it with such a range of differences that democratic governance becomes impossible to sustain.

Viewed in this way, the central question becomes one of finding a balance between the need for commonality in order to sustain the benefits of liberty and self-governance, and the need for difference in order to permit various cultures, languages, and value orientations to survive, perhaps even flourish and influence each other. How, for example, do we sustain the Latinos' interest in the Spanish language and a culture other than the dominant Anglo culture, while ensuring that there is sufficient commonality to sustain democratic governance? This same question might be raised for Native Americans, African Americans, Asian Americans, and many other racial and ethnic groups in the United States. It may also be framed in the context of gender, physical and mental condition, religious belief, sexual orientation, and age— all areas in addition to race and ethnicity where discriminatory practices have taken place.

Did you notice that last move? We shifted the ground from commonness and difference to that of discrimination. There is a connection, and it is critical to understanding the general concept of multiculturalism. In the multicultural context, discrimination occurs when people are treated differently because of such features as race, ethnicity, or gender, and this difference in treatment disadvantages those of a different race, ethnicity, or gender. What typically takes place here is that one group, let's call them the circles, says to the other group, the triangles, "We should hold certain things in common, such as language and traditions. If we do not hold these things in common, how can we hold our nation together?" The triangles respond with, "You circles have a point, but why must it be your language and your traditions? What's wrong with our language and traditions?" Just how this discourse plays out from here often depends, as the critical liberationists tell us, on which group is in power and which group is out of power. Critlibs speak often of hegemony and imperialism, wherein the group with power "colonizes" the groups lacking power.

A key point here is that to discriminate is to acknowledge difference in ways that disadvantage one group relative to another. To practice diversity is also to acknowledge difference, but without disadvantage to one group in relation to the other. On some occasions, diversity, or pluralism as it is sometimes known, may not only involve the absence of disadvantage, it might also include the presence of advantage to a group previously believed to have been disadvantaged by discrimination. Hence there are two separate questions that are part of the multicultural mix. The first is whether difference should be encouraged, and how doing so impacts the commonality believed necessary for democratic nationhood. The second is whether difference should result in advantage to one group over another, for the purpose of redressing past disadvantage. These two questions bear prominently in discussions of multiculturalism, but are often confused. The debate over bilingualism and race-centered schools of choice (such as public schools with an African-centered curriculum) are generally examples of the first, while the debate over affirmative action policies is generally an example of the second.

A paragraph back we described how the critlibs often view these disputes over multicultualism as exercises in power and domination. That the critilibs have a very central place in this discussion does not mean that the classlibs, executives, or fosterers are out of the multicultural loop. It has indeed been the case that the executives and the classlibs have not been engaged in the multicultural discussion to nearly the extent and intensity as the fosterers and the critlibs, but one should not infer from this that they are in opposition to multiculturalism. However, recall how important it is to the executive and classlib approaches to have a common base of knowledge and understanding (i.e., a clear, coherent x in the expression $T\phi Sxy$) and you will quickly gain an appreciation for how much of a challenge multiculturalism can be for executives and classlibs. Difference is a central feature of the fostering and critical liberation approaches, while commonness is central to the executive and classical liberation approaches. Fosterers and critlibs are not nearly so dependent on a carefully circumscribed body of knowledge and understanding, and thus experience less difficulty accommodating to rich conceptions of multiculturalism in their approaches to teaching. Executives and classlibs may also accommodate multiculturalism, although it requires more care and adaptation than is typically the case for fosterers and critlibs.

These variations in how the several approaches to teaching deal with key features of multiculturalism should lead us all to think carefully about the approach we take as teachers. Different approaches not only have different strengths and weaknesses; as we have seen, they also have different conse- quences for teachers and students. Thus one must be cautious about arguing that there is one right approach to teaching. A governing body would be well advised to avoid mandating one approach over another. If our excursion into the various approaches to teaching shows us anything, it is that the decision about approach must rest with teachers themselves, acting in concert and consultation with school administrators, boards, and parents. To mandate or legislate one approach over another is to favor certain conceptions of T, ϕ, S, x, and y over other conceptions, none of which may be in the best interests of this teacher, these learners, in this context, at this time. If, then, the decision ought to rest with the teacher, how does the teacher make this decision?

Deciding on an Approach

The answer to this question is not nearly so important to us as the question itself. The reason we value the question so much is that it contains what for us is a crucial point: You have a choice! What we want to emphasize is that in teaching, there are different ways to conceive of the relationship you forge with your students, there are different conceptions of what knowledge is and what is involved in you and your students knowing something, and there are different views of the point and purpose of teaching. If you are aware of and understand these different conceptions, you can "construct" an ap- proach to teaching that, in your considered judgment, best serves you and your students, your employer, and the parents of your students.

Too often, in our view, an approach to teaching is constructed by the cir- cumstances that teachers find as they prepare to teach. When this occurs, an approach "happens" to a teacher; it is not selected by a teacher after study and reflection. Our intent in developing these different approaches to teach- ing is to frame for you the possibility of selecting an approach to teaching that is grounded in the best ideas we have about what it means to participate in the education of the young. What you decide and how you decide are not nearly so important to us as *that* you decide—after becoming informed of the options and alternatives available to you, and formulating the very best set of reasons possible for why you choose to teach as you do.

If we reflect again on the provocative ideas of Kieran Egan, with which we began this chapter, it becomes obvious that these ideas are learner-focused; they emerge from a view of how human beings develop within the societies of which they are a part. Nothing wrong with that, except that there are at least two other powerful agents participating in the educational process, the teacher and the society. They, too, have needs and interests, which may not always mesh seamlessly with the needs and interests of the learner (which, as we have seen over and over in this book, vary depending on one's frame of reference). Consider another recent book, *The Courage to Teach* by Parker J. Palmer.[13] It carries the engaging subtitle, *Exploring the Inner Landscape of a Teacher's Life*. Palmer's argument is that truly superb teaching requires an integration of who and what we are with our methods and style of teaching (recall the discussion of manner in chapter 4). Hence who we are as teachers must make a difference to our teaching, just as who our students are must make a difference. Indeed, if we flesh this out a bit more, we think you will find that what we do as teachers is a blended influence of four factors: Self, Students, Content, and Context.

Each of us as teachers faces the very important challenge of constructing our pedagogy (a word more favored today than the term "approach") from elements of self, students, content, and context. In our experience, what too often happens is that a pedagogy is constructed with excessive attention on just one or two of these elements. Context is particularly powerful for many public school teachers, whose conceptions of what teaching is, and whose actual conduct as a teacher, are often strongly shaped by the structures and programs of the schools, and the expectations of parents, peers, and superiors, with too little regard to self or students, and perhaps content, too. What we have come to believe over these 15 years of wrestling with these ideas, and with you, our students, over these ideas, is that the important matter is not whether the approaches are compatible, or whether you are more of one approach than of the others, but that *you make conscious, thoughtful decisions about the kind of teacher you want to be, and that you remain reflective about the kind of teacher you are always in the process of becoming.* You will not, and indeed, should not, have total control of every aspect of your pedagogy. Parents, supervisors, and the state (as well as your students, of course) all have legitimate interests in your conduct as a teacher. However, it is your task not to let these legitimate interests shape your pedagogy as if it were some kind of putty. Your pedagogy should not happen to you; it should be constructed by you.

The approaches described in this book are tools, not templates. They are devices to aid your thinking about the teacher you wish to be, as well as the teacher you are in the process of becoming; they are not cookie cutters intended to shape you into being a teacher of a particular kind. If this book helps you to become that very special kind of reflective teacher, it will have fulfilled our fondest hopes. For the book, and for you.

Chapter 7

Cases and Disputes

To this point we have examined three approaches to teaching and have asked you to think about them along the way. They each have much to commend them, and yet each has potential negative features. To help you reflect on and develop your own examined approach to teaching, this last chapter contains a series of realistic vignettes—in the form of cases, dialogues, and disputes—that raise a number of issues, including ethical issues not dealt with extensively or directly in the text. As you read them and discuss them with others, you will have an opportunity to articulate and examine some of your most heartfelt beliefs about teaching. They will also give you the opportunity to bring theory and practice closer together by showing you that how one thinks about and approaches one's teaching makes a real difference in how one acts and reacts as a teacher in real-life situations.

To give you an overview of the topics we have treated and the major points at issue in them, we have provided a summary (see table 1) from which you can select cases and disputes of interest to you.

TABLE 1. Summary of Cases and Disputes

Page	Title*	Issue
82	Grading Policies (1)	Do different approaches call for different kinds of student evaluation?
84	An Educated Person (1)	What is essential to becoming truly educated?
85	School and Approach Mismatch (1)	Should a teacher change his or her approach to be more in line with school policies?
86	Teacher-Engineer or Artist? (2)	Is teaching an art or a science?
88	Individualized Learning (2)	Does research provide infallible material and techniques?

*A number in parentheses after a title indicates that the case or dispute is recommended for use with that specific chapter.

TABLE 1.   (*continued*)

Page	Title*	Issue
89	How Much Control Is Too Much? (2)	What are the advantages and disadvantages of the executive approach?
90	Workbook Dilemma (2)	Should the teacher or the administrator be the executive?
91	A New Science Kit (2)	Do curriculum materials reflect a technological mindset and limit teacher creativity?
92	Individual and Societal Needs (3)	Can the school serve both individual and social needs without conflict?
93	Curing Shyness (3)	Who determines the direction of personal growth, teacher or student?
94	What Standard Shall We Use? (3)	Should a teacher grade on personal growth and individual progress?
95	Teaching "Relevant" Literature (3)	What happens if students object to a teacher's approach?
96	Teacher and Mother? (3)	What happens if a teacher's personality and an approach do not fit?
97	Freedom and Indoctrination (4)	Can the mind ever really become free through education?
98	Too Young to Be Critical? (4)	Is developing a critical mind age related?
99	Education for Life (4)	Is a liberal education for everyone?
101	Freedom of Speech? (4)	How open-minded must a teacher using the liberationist approach be?
102	Mass or Class Culture? (4)	Is the liberationist approach elitist?
103	Learning Chemistry by Discussion (5)	Is the liberationist's manner efficient?
105	Different Learning Styles (5)	What factors decide choice of approach?
106	Compatibility of Approaches (5)	Must a teacher choose an approach?
107	Go Fly a Kite (1 and 5)	What happens when teachers use different approaches to the same school project?

Some of you may have already sampled these cases and disputes when following the suggestions we made throughout the text. To indicate our recommendations of issues related to specific chapters, we have placed a chapter number in parentheses following the title of each case or dispute. Of course, you should feel free to use them in any order suitable to your interests and purposes or to write your own cases and disputes that bring issues from your own experiences into your class discussions. Many of the cases and disputes in this chapter reach beyond the neat conceptual lines drawn around the three approaches described earlier in the text, demonstrating that the real world of education is not as neatly packaged as textbooks and scholars sometimes make it out to be. This is not to say that thinking initially about teaching in terms of the heuristic scheme of the three approaches dealt with in this book is useless. Rather, it is to warn that when theory and reality meet, you need to accommodate your categories and schemata to the world in which you live and work, making reasonable adjustments that will allow you to pursue your most basic beliefs and values. We also hope you will see that which name you give to your own approach to teaching is not as important as what you really believe about the purposes of teaching and what it means to be an educated person. Therefore, we hope you will use these cases and disputes as a bridge to the real world so that you may become a thinking and responsible teacher no matter what your approach.

Grading Policies

David Levine is the chairperson of Henry Hudson High School's Social Studies Department. Because of the size of the student population, several sections of certain courses are offered each year, and each is taught by a different instructor. In the case of Modern American History, three teachers offer courses. Students are assigned to these courses according to a simple alphabetical rotation. But this simple system has created a complex problem for Mr. Levine, for each teacher uses a different approach and parents and students are complaining that this is unfair.

The first section is taught by Albert Foley. Mr. Foley is a young, somewhat idealistic teacher who believes that stimulating learning experiences form the core of an education. In his class, he relies upon the study of current events from newspapers and television, and he encourages his students to initiate independent study projects. Mr. Foley is not as concerned about command of exact facts as he is about the personal significance that modern American history may come to hold for his students. In that direction, he believes, lies the promise of good citizenship and authentic personhood. Students are graded on the basis of essays they write about topics they select and journals of personal response to classroom discussion and current events. He grades because he has to, but he does not believe grading is what education is really about. Among the students, he is known as "Easy *A* Foley." In a typical year, 40 percent of his students will receive *A*'s and another 30 percent will receive *B*'s. The rest are given *C*'s, with an occasional *D* for serious cases. Mr. Foley says that any student will pass his class who is able to find his or her way to the classroom. In his opinion, it is hard enough being a teenager, and he is not going to make it any tougher. He believes that his students really learn and grow in their sense of self-worth because of his teaching and grading policies.

"Historical knowledge broadens and deepens the mind" might be the motto of Mr. William Sampson, the teacher of the second section, for he believes that history is all-important in getting students to understand the world they have inherited. Mr. Sampson uses textbooks containing primary sources, and he delivers detailed lectures. He demands that his students know the facts about American government and recent historical events, and he has little patience with uninformed opinion. He wants his students to use evidence from historical events and documents to back up their claims. In his view, good citizenship must rest on a sound foundation of knowledge and the ability to think critically. He tells his students that they will be graded on their ability to present sound arguments for their interpretations of historical events. His exams are not on the specific facts of history. Rather, he gives rigorous and demanding essay exams that force his students to think about history. In a recent class of forty students, Mr. Sampson's grades were distributed in the following manner: three *A*'s, five *B*'s, eighteen *C*'s, nine *D*'s, and five *F*'s. Mr. Sampson contends that his tests are fair measures of his students' ability to think. The students call him "Slasher Sampson."

Nancy Wright, the teacher of the third section, has taught history for twelve years, and each year she tries out new ideas and techniques she has read about in *Social Studies*, a national journal for teachers. This year she has developed a behavioral-objectives unit on the New Deal and has designed an evaluation instrument for it that gives her a very accurate assessment of a student's knowledge of FDR's policies. She has found that specifying her own objectives not only helps her but also helps her students see clearly what they need to study and learn in her classes. Each year she feels that her teaching is still improving. One thing she does not change, however, is her policy of grading according to a curve.

In her most recent group of forty students there were five *A*'s, ten *B*'s, fifteen *C*'s, seven *D*'s, and three *F*'s, a distribution of grades that she came to favor long ago after taking a course on statistics and evaluation. Ms. Wright uses both essays and objective tests designed by curriculum experts in order to provide an unbiased basis for her judgments. She believes that her proportional approach to grading accurately reflects the performance of each student as it compares to that of others in the class. Ms. Wright's students have no nickname for her.

Consider these different approaches to teaching and grading. Do you favor one over another? Why? Does each approach necessitate the kind of evaluation procedure used by each teacher, or could each use one another's grading policy without altering their approach very much? Does an approach also dictate the content in a course? Is this situation as it now exists fair to the students? What would you do if you were Mr. Levine?

An Educated Person

A: I was in my philosophy class today, and it really started me thinking about what it means to be a truly educated person.

B: It's really quite simple, isn't it? All that's required for becoming an educated person is graduation from a high school or a college.

A: It doesn't matter which? It doesn't matter what track or program or major you take?

B: No, it doesn't matter. Education is education, and each individual should have the kind of education he or she is best suited for. As long as a person learns what he or she is required to learn in order to graduate from whatever school, then in my book they're entitled to be called an educated person.

A: OK. Let's not argue about how much education you need or whether high school or college is sufficient. I don't think it's how long you go to school that counts anyway, as much as what you learn. But according to you, it doesn't even matter *what* you study or learn as long as you graduate from somewhere. Well, suppose there was a school where only math was taught. Would a person who only learned math and didn't know much about other things like history or science or art really be an educated person?

B: I see what you mean. That might be too narrow an education. I just mean that to really be educated, people should study what they are best suited for. They should be allowed to develop their own unique potential and identity. That's what being properly educated is all about; of course, you have to study other things so your education won't be too narrow. All schools and colleges require that, don't they?

A: That's just the point. It's the "other things" that make you a truly *educated* person. What you learn for yourself helps you become the unique *person* you will be, but what you learn in common with others is what makes you *educated*. So the problem is what "other things" does everyone need to study to become educated persons.

B: Math, history, literature, science, art—you know—the basic subjects.

A: And if you really learn them, then you're educated?

B: Of course.

A: Even if you never learned to care about other people or to be honest or fair? Is learning subjects all that education is about or is being educated and becoming an educated person more than that?

B: What more is there?

What do you think? To what degree is becoming educated developing one's unique potential and to what degree is it learning common things so that we can share and participate in our common cultural heritage as equals? Is there more to it than either of these two things?

School and Approach Mismatch

Janet had taught history for several years at a junior college. Tired of lecturing and longing for a change, she decided to try working at a different level in the education system. The public schools were not hiring, so she accepted a job with a small, conservative, church-affiliated secondary school at a considerable reduction in salary, even though she was neither conservative nor religious. She agreed to teach four sections of freshman history and one of remedial junior English, with a total of 143 students.

Janet found teaching high school challenging and exciting. She liked being with the students and even relished lunchroom duty, because it afforded her the opportunity to observe student interaction and to interact herself. Accustomed to dealing with adults and high school graduates, she treated her students with respect and genuine care. In a short time she developed an easy relationship with her classes and became known as an adult who could be approached. Janet made a habit of coming to work early every day in order to be available for those students who wanted to shoot the breeze or needed to talk seriously.

There was usually someone waiting for her, occasionally a student other than one of her own or even a fellow teacher.

As much as she loved and was rewarded by her work, she found dealing with the school's administration to be very difficult. Janet's personal philosophy of education emphasized discovery, opening the world for the student. She attempted to create a proper relaxed atmosphere for this. The school's position stressed adherence to rules, deference to authority, and strict norms of acceptable behavior. There was a rigid curriculum that was to be dispensed by the teacher and learned by the students. Teachers were responsible for seeing to it that all students learned this material. A proper distance between teacher and students was always to be maintained.

Janet soon found herself in conflict with the administration over these policies. Each classroom had a two-way speaker, and it was known that the principal and the attendance secretary occasionally listened in on class sessions. During the third week of school, Janet had been called on the carpet for allowing excessive noise in her classroom. When she apologized to her neighbors, she discovered that the complaint had not come from them but from the attendance secretary, who had been eavesdropping on the public-address system. Her colleagues also told her that the principal was dissatisfied because she was not covering the prescribed curriculum. Janet was furious about the way her teaching had been "observed."

Janet obviously faced a year at school in which she would often be acting in ways directly opposed to administrative goals and philosophy. But she needed her job.

In light of that economic reality, ought Janet to change her approach to teaching to be more in line with the administration's? Might it be possible to find a compromise approach? Should a teacher compromise his or her approach when it does not match the school's philosophy? What about professional autonomy and integrity? Do you think the "observation system" in this school is proper? What would you do if you were Janet?

Teacher—Engineer or Artist?

A: The practical importance of science is clear. It provides us with knowledge we can use in curing diseases, in exploring space, and in helping students learn. Education, no less than medicine or space exploration, must rest on a solid foundation of knowledge about how to do it.

B: I don't deny that knowledge about teaching like time on-task or how to design valid multiple-choice questions can be useful to a teacher. But when you come right down to it, teaching is an art. You can know your subject matter and materials, have a good grasp of learning theory and methods, and know the latest research findings, but when you're there in the classroom, your performance has to be more like an artist's than like a mechanical engineer's. Each teacher is a unique person, and it is by being yourself that you really become a good teacher.

A: A good teacher is an effective teacher, a teacher whose students learn! That can only happen if you think about your goals, carefully plan your lessons, select the appropriate techniques you will use, and exercise good judgment as you're teaching. If that is like being an *engineer*, so be it. It's not your artistic uniqueness that's important, it's your knowledge, experience, and executive ability that counts.

B: But what about those unanticipated teachable moments, those unplanned things the teacher as artist does that really get students excited about learning? What makes teaching come alive is the artistic talent of the really good teacher, not what he or she knows about the "science of teaching."

C: You both make good points. I'm not sure you really can separate the artistic from the scientific in any serious human endeavor. The good surgeon is as much artist as scientist and so is the good teacher.

A: If, by calling a surgeon an artist, you mean that he effectively executes his skills, I would agree. But that just makes my point. Both the surgeon and teacher depend on the knowledge gained through research that proves one technique or method better than another, more effective in curing patients or in getting students to learn. It is the scientific knowledge that makes it possible to get the best results.

B: But don't you see what you're both assuming, that a better teacher is simply one who *produces* more learning regardless of subject matter and regardless of effects on students. That's a one-sided, mechanical view of teaching. An artistic view seeks to make the educational experience of students more self-fulfilling, more personally relevant, and more satisfying, and only a sensitive artist can do that.

A: Would you rather be evaluated as a teacher on an agreed-upon set of competencies you are expected to demonstrate by means of an instrument developed and validated for the purpose—or by some "art critic" supervisor who may or may not like your brand of art?

How would you prefer to be evaluated as a teacher? As an artist? As an engineer? Do you think that someone who takes the executive approach to teaching is less inclined to see things other than learning goals as important in teaching? What might such other things be?

Individualized Learning

Bob was a first-year teacher in a fifth-grade open classroom. Bob, like all the other teachers of his teaching team, had responsibility for one homogeneously grouped math class. The math program of the school was designed according to the latest research in the following manner: Each student progressed through a series of worksheets; when one worksheet was finished correctly, the student went to the next. In this way, skill in addition, subtraction, multiplication, and other areas was to be learned at an individual's own pace. The idea was that the teacher could give individual attention to those children who needed it. Research had shown that at this grade level individualization was most effective.

Bob thought this system made sense. The students seemed to like the class, too. They were rewarded by the evidence of their progress and by the praise Bob gave when papers were completed.

Before long, though, Bob began to be uneasy about the direction his math class was taking. He felt that he was not really "teaching" his students. They were just doing worksheets on their own. He had thought he would be able to work one-on-one with the children. Instead, he found he spent almost no time with anyone. There was constantly a line of five or six children either waiting to ask questions or waiting to have papers checked. Bob felt that he could not afford to give as much time to each child as he would have liked, since it would be unfair to keep all the others waiting. The children who finished papers were congratulated and sent on to the next worksheet. The students who had questions were told to try to work out an answer by themselves. They often would, but this usually took the form of three or four unsuccessful guesses before the correct answer was stumbled upon. Furthermore, Bob was so busy at his desk that he had difficulty being sure students were working and behaving as they should. Some students seemed to be progressing much too slowly. Bob was concerned that this was because he had not watched these pupils closely enough. In short, Bob came to see himself less as a teacher and more as a "paper pusher."

Bob's worst fears seemed to be realized one day when he held an addition game. Bob chose problems that all the students should have known, since they came from worksheets all the students had completed. Contrary to Bob's expectations, many of his students were unable to do the problems he chose. It appeared that, indeed, many of Bob's students were not learning.

If you were Bob, what would you do? Do you think that Bob, knowingly or not, was using a teacher-as-executive approach here? Did his approach cause the problem and/or did it help him diagnose the problem? Why do you think research showed one thing about individualization and Bob found another? Was Bob really teaching?

How Much Control Is Too Much?

Elsie Simmons, a new teacher, was having second thoughts about the way she was teaching her junior literature class. At the start of the school year, her principal and colleagues had told her that the students she was getting were a rambunctious group—bright and eager, but in need of firm control. This, plus the fact that Elsie was a beginning teacher, had prompted the advice that Elsie exercise decisive control over the group from day one. Otherwise, they would take advantage of Elsie's inexperience. Research has shown that this technique produces the desired results.

Elsie took their suggestion to heart. She prepared meticulous lesson plans so that the class periods would always be under her control. And she stuck to these. The students were given specific readings to do and lists of questions to answer. During class, Elsie saw to it that she was always in charge, either through lecturing or directing questions to students.

As she looked back on things, Elsie saw that her teaching had been successful in one respect—the students were not behavior problems. The trouble was that they were too passive. They did not seem to "get into" the material. Elsie saw none of the enthusiasm and creative energy that this group was noted for and that they demonstrated in their other classes. At best, the class's work was adequate. In addition, Elsie was upset that many of the students seemed to resent her.

Elsie had hoped to make the literature course one where students could exchange ideas and express themselves. It did not seem to be working that way. Though she knew she would like to alter things, Elsie was not sure how or whether this could be done at this point. What should she do?

How might this teacher modify her approach? What are the pluses and minuses of an executive approach? Is this approach inappropriate for Elsie, or is it the way Elsie had implemented it that is at fault? Was this form of the executive approach a necessary first tactic?

Workbook Dilemma

Julie Karajian is a kindergarten teacher. She is considered one of the best teachers at P.S. 21, and in fact has been the subject of a documentary for network television and several articles on teacher excellence in various publications. Her philosophy of teaching is that children learn from experimentation and exploration. From this approach, Julie believes, children derive knowledge from relevant experiences and also develop an essential self-confidence needed to master future skills. Julie adapts each year's curriculum according to the type of class that enters in September. Activities reflect the group's unique learning styles. Julie is not a firm believer in the use of workbooks and learning kits, unless they are directly relevant to the children's abilities and backgrounds, which Julie has found they usually are not.

Mr. Jackson is the principal of P.S. 21. He is more interested in controlling the students in his school than anything else. He does not see children as unique individuals with specific styles of learning. Rather, he believes that most children fit into two categories: bright and not bright. He thinks teachers need to mold the children to a particular methodology, rather than vice versa. He is aware of the diverse cultures from which his students come, but he believes that in order to survive in the real world children in this school must learn to get along as adaptive adults. He is also confident that workbooks and learning kits serve two significant functions in his school: to control students by keeping them busy and to serve as guidelines for what gets taught.

Recently, however, he has been approached by Julie concerning her class's new workbooks. She believes that because of their age level, developmental level, and cultural backgrounds, these children will find the workbooks stifling and irrelevant. Instead of using them for a total of two hours a week as required, Julie proposes not to use them at all. Mr. Jackson recognizes Julie as the best in the school, but he firmly believes these children need to become familiar with workbook usage and that use of the workbooks will teach them skills necessary for success in first grade. At the same time, he knows that children who come out of Julie's class often do the best in the first grade, so maybe they do not need the books as much. Besides, he has heard that Julie is tired of battling the administration and is thinking of moving to a private school. If she does, P.S. 21 will lose its greatest asset. But if the other kindergarten teachers find out that she is not using her workbooks, they will undoubtedly be angered that they are required to do so. Furthermore, what if Julie's children do not learn the necessary skills because they are unfamiliar with workbooks?

What should Mr. Jackson do? Is there some sort of compromise that could be reached? What should Julie do, as the teacher who knows her children best and who is confident about her approach to teaching? Should the teacher or the administrator be the executive?

A New Science Kit

It was the first teacher preparation day of the new school year, and Emma Dill was in her fifth-grade classroom unpacking the new materials that had arrived for her during the summer. After finding places for the paper clips, thumb tacks, and new construction paper, Emma turned to the gem of her shipment, a new science kit.

The district curriculum director, in consultation with a committee of principals and teachers, had decided on the new science curriculum to replace the textbook series that previously had been used throughout the district. Emma had served on the committee and had enthusiastically supported the choice.

Emma was one of those teachers who enjoyed teaching science. She never considered it a "filler" to finish out the last twenty or so minutes of the day. She always allotted plenty of time for science. She scheduled as many experiments as possible.

The main selling point of the new kit was that it involved experiments almost exclusively. Furthermore, all the materials except for a few common consumables were included in the kit, no small consideration in light of the time and energy Emma had spent collecting the things needed for experiments suggested by the old science text or developed by Emma herself. Even further, Emma had noted to herself with a certain amount of glee, all those teachers who had refused to do the experiments Emma considered so vital to the study of science would no longer have a way to avoid doing them.

Unfortunately (fortunately?), however, Emma had taken a summer workshop on school and society and had learned of neo-Marxist criticisms of schools. Neo-Marxists argued that the schools reproduced working-class mindsets in the children, and at the time she wondered if that really could be true. As she looked through the science kit now, she felt her enthusiasm for it wane. The kit consisted of several units. Each unit was comprised of a series of activity cards stating the purpose, materials, procedure, and questions for each activity. There were five copies of each activity card, so that several small groups of students could all work at once, moving in order through each step. There was a basic serial organization of the activities and units, and it was essential to do all activities in one unit before moving to the next. Students were to be rewarded in terms of the number of units completed. Emma reflected that these features, which last spring had appeared to her to offer opportunities for experimentation, pupil involvement, and pupil self-direction, now appeared different. She wondered whether the sources of the virtue of the kits—organization and self-sufficiency—represented hidden liabilities. The kit stressed pupils' following directions over personal interaction with the teacher, prescribed goals over goals developed by the teacher and the class, following a recipe over developing a method, and so on. In short, Emma was troubled by the thought that rather than giving her students an exciting encounter with science, she was really instilling technobureaucratic values, just as the neo-Marxist theorists warned.

Do you think Emma has accurately assessed the situation? Are her fears justified? Should she use the kit? Do curriculum materials based on an executive approach to teaching reflect a technological mindset and limit teacher creativity?

Individual and Societal Needs

A: Think about it; each of us has only one life to live. Education should help each person make his or her life meaningful and fulfilling as an individual. You can't do that by forcing students to learn what they don't find personally meaningful just because it happens to be in the curriculum guide.

B: What would you teach them then?

A: It's not *what* you teach that's really important. Don't you see? It is helping children and adolescents become themselves. Too many students just pass through the system and get treated in a mechanical way as we sort and train them for meaningless jobs and empty lives in our materialistic society. We should help them become their own unique selves.

B: That sounds good, but did you ever try to run an office or a factory full of "own unique selves"? There's nothing wrong with being yourself on your own time, but when it comes to being a productive member of society, that takes cooperation and subordination of personal concerns for the greater good of all.

A: In the long run, the greater good of all depends on achieving the greater good for each individual, and that is becoming a well-adjusted, self-accepting, emotionally stable person. If our educational system could do that, nothing else would be needed.

B: What about reading, writing, and arithmetic? And what about producing doctors, lawyers, teachers, and all the educated persons required for our high-tech workforce? Be realistic, life is not always just being yourself. Each of us has to be something society needs. Schools are society's instruments for providing primarily for society's needs and only secondarily for the needs of individuals.

What do you think? What is the first obligation of the schools and their teachers, to the individual or to society? Are the views of *A* and *B* necessarily incompatible? Can both societal and individual needs be met at the same time, or is some subordination of one to the other always necessary?

Curing Shyness

Jill Yablonski was concerned about Tom, a student in her fourth-grade class. Tom was one of those shy children who always seemed to be on the fringe of things. At recess, he usually played by himself. In class, he preferred to sit quietly and listen. He did not initiate exchanges with other students or with Jill. It was not that Tom was sullen. In fact, he was a pleasant child; it was just that he liked to keep to himself. His school work was good. The other children did not dislike him particularly, although they rarely associated with him. In short, Tom did not seem to be suffering from his shyness. His previous teachers all said that Tom had always been shy but had done well for them. But Jill was not satisfied with this. She thought Tom had just been ignored. Jill thought she ought to do something to help Tom learn to interact with other people.

She set about getting Tom involved. She got other children to play with him. She had Tom lead class discussions. Tom acquiesced in these activities without comment, and he seemed to handle them pretty well. Jill hoped this meant Tom was making progress.

Thus she was rather surprised when she received a note from Tom's parents, who said that Tom had become very unhappy about school. Where before Tom had always been eager to tell his day's experiences, lately he came close to tears and was unwilling to talk when asked about school. Tom's parents asked whether Jill had any idea what the problem was.

Jill did have an idea. She suspected that her program of personal growth and socialization was at the root of the matter. She was disturbed that Tom was unhappy; he had seemed to do well. She was not at all sure she should desist, though. It might be difficult in the short term, but considered in a larger perspective, Tom ought to get over his shyness. It would be a handicap later. On the other hand, maybe she was pushing things. Maybe Tom would grow out of it on his own. Maybe he was simply a shy person.

What should Jill do? Should she change her approach? Is she correct in her diagnosis of Tom? Does taking a therapist approach to teaching mean leading a child to a goal perceived by the teacher as growth? Or does it mean permitting the child to grow in his own way? Does Jill have the right to make Tom unhappy for "his own good"? When, if ever, is intrusion in the personal development of others justified?

What Standard Shall We Use?

The faculty of Craigsdale High School is in an uproar. Susan Salerno, a new member of the faculty, has been raising questions at faculty meetings that strike at many long-held assumptions about the aims and policies of education. It all revolves around her grading policy. Susan believes that it is not fair to use a single standard of evaluation to grade all students in a class regardless of ability or level at which they begin. Such a system, she says, is not pedagogically tenable. Education aims at the growth of persons and must necessarily start at whatever level the student is at and reflect what that person is capable of achieving. A single standard against which all are graded is an externally imposed criterion that cannot measure personal growth. Further, such a standard distinguishes those who succeed from those who fail by creating failure even when a student may be doing his or her best. This system is especially untenable now that classes at Craigsdale are increasingly heterogeneous but cannot be justified even if that were not the case.

Early in the term, Susan asked her students to do a project. After giving them a grade for it and copious comments and suggestions for improvements, she had them redo the project for the end of the term. Students were then graded on how much they had improved from their first project. A student going from failing work to a C may get an A for the course. This procedure, Susan believes, more fairly evaluates student achievement and more adequately reflects what they have *learned*.

Susan's colleagues are not convinced. One of them, Tom Abelson, argues that education has traditionally been involved with setting standards of excellence for students to aspire to. Such standards are public measures of competence, and all students should be accountable to them. Ellen Myers adds that schools are expected to grade according to such a uniform standard. A system like Susan's throws into doubt the value of students' grades when they compete for scholarships or apply to schools of higher learning.

Susan replies to Tom that she *is* using a standard of excellence to assess student achievement. She evaluates their projects according to rigorous standards of excellence. However, when it comes to evaluating the *progress* students have made over the semester, she believes that they can only be their own measure of achievement.

To Ellen, Susan responds that it is unfortunate that the educational system is organized to a large extent the way she describes. However, that is no reason for continuing to use a policy that is pedagogically unjustified—in essence, having students compete according to a standard that may be inappropriate for them. Education should be about each person growing according to his or her own needs and abilities. Besides, grades often reflect the evaluation systems of individual teachers and are not comparable from school to school.

The case is not closed. What would you add to the continuing dialogue at Craigsdale? (Role playing might be useful here.) Does Susan have a point about the personal progress aspect of education? Is it fair or educative to evaluate students using a uniform standard of achievement? On the other hand, can we ignore public measures of educational success or failure? Should there be standards by which all are graded? What do you think?

Teaching "Relevant" Literature

Today had been a big day for Jennifer Calhoun. For the first time as a student teacher she had taken over the junior literature classes in which she had been observing. Jennifer had put a great deal of thought into the unit on twentieth-century American literature she was to teach for the next six weeks. The progressive theorists she had been reading about in her foundation course at State College greatly influenced her thinking, so she aimed to make the students themselves the center of her unit. She was not so concerned that the students learn to analyze literature; she wanted them to be excited by their work, enjoy their readings, and take away something meaningful from the class. In Jennifer's opinion, these things had not happened in the class up to that time.

So Jennifer spent a great deal of time developing a reading list that would be appealing and relevant to the students. She chose stories, poems, and books about teenagers, and some were even written by young people. Because the student population was diverse, she chose works by authors of different ethnic and racial backgrounds, too. The activities she developed concentrated on free discussion and creative writing assignments. She really wanted the students to become engaged with literature in a way that would help them to see themselves and to develop as persons; she structured her curriculum accordingly.

Armed with her enthusiasm and thoughtfully developed plan for meeting her goals, Jennifer introduced her unit to the classes (and to her supervisor, who was observing that day). But against her expectations, the students did not seem to be particularly excited by the readings and activities that Jennifer presented. Some even objected to them.

That afternoon, when discussing the day with her supervisor, Jennifer frankly admitted that she was puzzled and dejected by the students' reactions to her unit. The advice her supervisor offered puzzled Jennifer even more.

Her supervisor told her that by this time students were pretty set in their ways and new approaches were perceived as threatening. Also, in this junior class, many students were looking to apply to colleges. They knew that PSATs, SATs, and achievement tests were right around the corner and that standard questions on the literature sections would not be about the books on Jennifer's list. The supervisor advised Jennifer to return to the standard curriculum and standard assignments and tests. It was only fair to her students not to change things.

What would you do if you were Jennifer? Can and should the system and situational realities restrict the degree of freedom a teacher has in choosing an approach? What do you think?

Teacher and Mother?

Susie Simon was a new fifth-grader in Westville Elementary School. Eight months before, Susie's mother had been killed in a traffic accident. Susie's father was concerned that Susie needed the attention of female adults. Susie missed her mother very much, and Mr. Simon felt that he was unable to fill the roles of both father and mother. For that reason, when he enrolled Susie in Westville, he asked that she be placed in Michelle Saint Martin's class rather than in that of Mike Walsh, the other fifth-grade teacher. The principal assented to the request.

When Michelle met with her principal, he explained Mr. Simon's request. Susie needed a female role model, he said. She needed a woman to talk to and to listen to her problems. She needed affection.

Michelle listened with sympathy, but she was uneasy. She was not sure she could, or should, take on this responsibility. She had thirty-one other students in her class. Her time and energy were already extended to the limit. She could not see how she would be able to give Susie the individual attention she needed. Besides, Michelle just was not a "huggy" sort of person. Other teachers felt comfortable with overtly showing affection; but not Michelle. That was not her temperament. Anyway, she did not believe such relationships were in a student's best interests. Sure, her colleagues chided her for being too straight-laced, but none doubted her skill and commitment to teaching. Weren't those the important things, after all?

Michelle wished she could help Susie. But she was not sure the principal's way was the right way. She could be a good teacher for Susie, but she could not replace her mother. Michelle had the feeling that trying to force herself to be somebody she wasn't would be hypocritical and might lead to resentment. She did not want to do anything to harm Susie. What should she do?

Is parenting a proper component of teaching? Is the principal putting unreasonable demands on Michelle by asking her to change her approach in this case? Should she try to show more affection in her teaching? Are there ways to show it without making undue emotional or physical demands? What can be done to serve the best interests of Susie and the other students? What would you do if you were in Michelle's place?

Freedom and Indoctrination

A: We all grow up in the narrow world of our parents and friends, a small place where their views, beliefs, and values become ours through the process sociologists call primary socialization. Education gives us the opportunity to free ourselves from the accident of our birth in a particular time, place, and family. It broadens our horizons and helps us to become members of the family of man.

B: But there are many families of man. There are different nations and different cultures, and that means education can't help but be indoctrination into one's national or cultural frame of mind. You may escape the narrow confines of the family you are born into through schooling, but you just trade that in for a narrow nationalistic or cultural bias. No mind can really be free. Education is a form of indoctrination.

A: Indoctrination means being taught things as if they were unquestionably true. In America, we teach people that it's all right to question, to challenge authority on logical, moral, or other reasonable grounds. Freedom is not only being allowed to do that; in a democracy it is also learning the skills needed to do it well. Learning to be a critical thinker is what a liberal education should be about. Then we ourselves can determine truth and falsity, good and evil, and not behave like unthinking sheep in a herd.

B: But a critical thinker can challenge everything and anything, right? Then even the idea of a liberal education can be challenged! And what about traditional values, beliefs, and norms? Isn't anything sacred or just plain worth not challenging because it is appreciated, it is valued, it is "our way"? Must everything be either true or false, right or wrong when challenged by the critical thinker? Like Atlas holding up the world on his shoulders, you have to be able to stand on something.

A: That something is our belief in reason, in having good evidence for our claims, in open-mindedness, and in critical thinking.

B: But aren't those ideas just part of the Western liberal culture as it evolved over the last three hundred years? Other cultures believe in authority and tradition, in group solidarity rather than rugged individualism. Besides, even our so-called forms of knowledge are based on conceptualizations of experience that are culture-laden. There's no way for a mind, initiated into the knowledge base of a culture, to be free.

What do you think? Is a liberationist approach to teaching possible? Can a person learn to overcome cultural biases? To what extent can education free the mind and to what extent must education be indoctrination?

Too Young to Be Critical?

Li Nguyen had some definite ideas about the aims of his junior high social studies class. He wanted his students to be politically aware and able to free themselves from the domination of political sloganeering.

Li proposed to accomplish this through critical inquiry in the social studies. In his class, the emphasis was on giving reasons for beliefs. Unsubstantiated claims were subjected to criticism. Critical, reasoned thought was the theme of his teaching.

Li was beginning to think his class was really achieving his aim when he was called into the principal's office. The principal told Li that she had received several complaints from parents that their children had come home advocating provocative and objectionable opinions on political and social issues. This situation was unsatisfactory to the parents not only because of the content of their children's opinions but because of the way they were held. Several of the parents complained that the children would not listen to them when they gave counterarguments. The children said that Mr. Nguyen told them they had a right to their own opinions in these matters. The parents demanded immediate change. Some had gone so far as to imply that, because of his background as a political refugee, Li was not motivated by scholarship but by self-serving concerns.

The principal asked Li to meet later with her and a few of the parents in order to explain his program. Li went back to his room to consider the principal's news. He resented the implication that he was selfishly motivated. But how was he to justify his approach? He was not sure that the situation was a bad one. He felt that perhaps rebellion was a necessary first step toward critical thinking. And he believed that children *did* have a right to question accepted beliefs. On the other hand, he was disturbed that some students were unwilling to listen to their parents' arguments. He had stressed the value of an open mind. Class discussions had emphasized the need to listen to others and give good reasons for one's own beliefs. The students had seemed to learn that lesson. What should Li do? What would you say to the parents if you were Li?

Are there ages where a liberationist approach might be inappropriate? If so, is the problem in the manner generally, or can a valid liberationist approach still be developed for any age group? Irrespective of age, to what extent is a liberationist approach appropriate for teaching if it brings a community's values into question?

Education for Life

P: If we have learned anything from the past, it's that we cannot predict the future. Before the twentieth century, atom splitting was considered impossible, and no one could possibly have anticipated the problems of nuclear waste or nuclear war. Therefore, educators cannot be content to teach what we think we now know. We must prepare people for the future by teaching them how to think and how to solve problems.

T: Problem solving is important, of course, and the future can't be known, that's true. But I believe that the best way to be prepared to face the future is with a rich knowledge of what human beings have come to know about themselves and their world and not just with some skills of critical thinking. In fact, critical thinking is best taught through a study of science, philosophy, and even art. These critical ways of thinking that are imbedded in our cultural heritage must be passed on by learning these subjects.

P: No, critical thinking and problem-solving skills are best learned, not through books and lectures on traditional subjects, but through experimentation and successful adaptations in real-life situations. Too much of schooling is a pedantic worshipping of traditions removed from the real world. No wonder students see little connection between life and what they learn in school. We must make learning meaningful, and that can only happen if people are not forced to study things disconnected from their lives but are given the opportunity to study what interests them.

T: But students are too young to know what's meaningful. We adults are better judges of what will be the rich rewards of a solid classical education. Interests can be fickle in youth. What's relevant today may not be so tomorrow. The wisdom of the past is always relevant.

P: Let's get down to brass tacks! What butcher or barber needs to know algebra or physics? What policeman, Shakespeare, or nurse, philosophy? What ordinary people need to know is how to solve *real* problems, how to be good workers, good parents, and good citizens. Your education is for an elite, not for good, ordinary people.

T: You are so shortsighted! Good and productive lives are lived by people who are enriched by their education and not just taught how to do this or that. You would give people less than they deserve in the name of practical utility. I offer them their share of their rich cultural inheritance.

How do you react to this debate? Can critical thinking and problem-solving skills be taught apart from the liberal arts and sciences? Is a traditional curriculum the best preparation for life? Does a liberationist approach require both certain subject matters and certain skills? What do you think?

Freedom of Speech?

Joan Wagner has taught American history and government at Ringwood High School for fifteen years. Her students and colleagues consider Joan to be a fair and popular teacher. In her classroom she encourages her students to voice their opinions and to keep open minds. She insists that each student receive a fair hearing from the other students. On her part, Joan feels that it is important that she not impose her opinion on her students. It would be too easy, and unfair, to push her point of view successfully, taking advantage of her popularity and position of authority. Moreover, she would not want to humiliate students who have expressed different points of view. But most importantly, Joan would not impose her opinion because that would run counter to her goals as a teacher—to foster students' critical capabilities and to encourage them to participate in our democratic system of government.

Tommy Jones comes to class one day with a swastika drawn on his arm and a KKK leaflet taped to his notebook. Joan does not notice at first, but her attention is drawn to them during the course of the day because a black boy, Steven, and a Jewish girl, Rachel, approach him individually about them. Being the only black and the only Jew in the class, they are both too self-conscious to make an issue of them. Joan decides she has to talk to Tommy.

Joan has Tommy meet her after class the next day. Tommy is still sporting his swastika and KKK leaflet and makes it abundantly clear that he knows what the swastika and the KKK represent. In fact, he has read some literature, attended a KKK meeting, and thought the matter through carefully. He has decided that white Americans must protect themselves against Jews and blacks.

When Joan asks Tommy, please, not to come to class with such symbols, he asserts that he has freedom of speech and that he is merely expressing an informed opinion, as Joan has urged her students to do. Tommy says that he does not intend to get violent with Steven or Rachel. In response to Joan's suggestion that the beliefs of the Nazis and the KKK are offensive and threatening to Steven and Rachel even if he does not intend to hurt them physically, Tommy replies that the beliefs of blacks and Jews are threatening to white Christian Americans. Moreover, people have pro-abortion and antinuclear stickers on their notebooks. Would Joan ask those students not to come to class with those stickers because they are offensive to Tommy?

The next day, Tommy comes to class with the swastika and the leaflet in place. Joan later hears from a counselor that Steven's and Rachel's parents have suggested that they will have their children switch classes if nothing is done.

Should Joan insist that Tommy not come to class with the swastika and KKK leaflet? Should she defend Tommy's freedom of speech and suggest that Rachel's and Steven's parents likewise can exercise their freedom by switching their children's classes? Should Joan stand by while Tommy learns that he can be victorious and powerful with his swastika, since he and others might know why Steven and Rachel have left the class? Can Joan impose her opinion without countering the rules of her class, abandoning her liberationist approach, and exposing a student to humiliation? Can she raise this issue like any other issue in class, not knowing what the outcome will be as well as forcing Steven and Rachel to defend themselves? What do you think?

Mass or Class Culture?

A: Everybody complains about school being separate from life, but nobody does anything about it! Students are forced to read Shakespeare when in real life no one needs to force them to read comics and racy novels. They're forced to listen to symphonies and opera when in real life rock and country music sing to them. Art isn't in museums, but all around them in advertising and in the design of useful and beautiful products. Even our modern artists, the soup-can and comic-strip painters, saw that! Why do we persist in trying to initiate students into an artifically esoteric culture when their own real culture is so rich and satisfying? Why not help them critically engage in their culture of the real world and have school make a difference in their lives?

B: Because Shakespeare, Beethoven, and Rembrandt do make a difference in the lives of all of us. They represent some of the heights human beings have achieved, and their works speak eloquently to universal human emotions and feelings in ways barely plumbed in the pop culture. Why use mediocre examples to teach aesthetic and humane sensitivity when models of excellence are there for the taking?

A: Because students won't take them! Because students feel that their art forms are not appreciated by us. In fact, we make them feel as if their genuinely felt appreciation for their literature, art, movies, and music is a low form of uncultured, adolescent emotionalism, a phase one might have to go through but should grow out of. We treat as trivial and meaningless what they take very seriously as meaningful, as reflecting their deepest-felt emotions and needs.

B: Emotions are not what culture and art forms are about. It is intellect in its highest form that creates culture. The business of the school is developing intellect, not pampering the emotions. Television provides all the emotion, base action, and nonintellectual stimulation students need and then some. We need to counterbalance such negative cultural forces.

A: Why negative? Why must what speaks to masses of good, hardworking, plain people be negative and what speaks to only a few who see themselves as an elite be positive? Our levels of intellectual ability may differ, but all humans share the same emotional capacities to feel love, anger, empathy, caring, and joy. Our curriculum should capitalize on this capacity and use the common art forms of everyday life to bridge the gap between school and life and teach our youth about the common humanity of all human beings.

B: You win. Let's get rid of all the literature books from the storeroom and library and replace them with comics and drugstore paperbacks in our English courses. Let's clean out those old-fashioned instruments and classical records from the music room and replace them with guitars, electronic sound enhancement paraphernalia, and the latest pop records. As for art, let's . . .

A: Wait a minute, we don't have to go that far, do we?

What do you think? Does popular culture have a place in the curriculum? Does teaching high culture make students feel that their culture is inferior? Is it? Is the liberationist approach elitist?

Learning Chemistry by Discussion

Mr. Tanaka's high school chemistry class had been studying how chemical elements and compounds have unique physical properties such as solubility and density. Most recently, the students had observed in experiments how compounds show characteristic melting and freezing points. When compounds were heated and the temperatures graphed in relation to time, the students discovered that plateaus occur as the compounds change physical state from solid to liquid and from liquid to gas, and that these plateaus occur at different temperatures for different substances.

Today, Mr. Tanaka presented a problem to his students. He explained that he had been filling a container with a colorless liquid before class and had been called away to receive a phone call. When he returned, he continued filling the container, but with a different colorless liquid that he had taken up by mistake. The container sat on his desk. Mr. Tanaka asked if anyone in the class could think of a way to separate the two liquids so that the accidental mixture would not have to be thrown out.

After good naturedly reprimanding Mr. Tanaka for making such a careless error, the class began to think about the problem. There followed a lively discussion.

Art: That's a hard problem. I can see how one could separate marbles, say, but those are big and easy to see. Molecules are too tiny to separate.

Bernice: Maybe the liquids will separate themselves, like oil and water do.

Mr. Tanaka: Not a bad idea, Bernice. That's a technique that might work sometimes. Unfortunately, these chemicals mix completely.

Conrad: I don't know how this might work, but we've learned how molecules of different compounds behave differently. Could we use that fact somehow?

Dawn: I think Conrad is on to something there. Maybe we can't pick out molecules like marbles, but there could be some way that we could make the molecules sort themselves out.

Edgar: That's right. Like when we used filters to separate precipitates from liquids.

Mr. Tanaka: You've given some good ideas! There are filtering-like techniques, called chromatography, which can be used to separate liquids. We'll discuss that later. Can anyone think of other ways to make molecules separate themselves?

Fran: Compounds are different in how they respond to heating. Can we use that?

Mr. Tanaka: What do the rest of you think? What have we learned about heating compounds?

Grace: Well, we know that there are plateaus in the temperature-time graph where the compound changes its physical state. And different compounds have different freezing and boiling points.

Hector: I have an idea! If we heat the mixture, would one compound boil off first?

Ingrid: But how could you catch the gas that was boiled off?

Julio: What happens to the boiling points when compounds are mixed, though? Wouldn't the mixture have its own boiling point?

Mr. Tanaka: I'm pleased that you all have learned so much! Ingrid and Julio, you've raised some important problems we have to think about, but Hector is on the right track. We *can* use the difference in boiling points of some compounds to separate them when they are mixed.

This isn't always easy, for there are complications, just as Ingrid and Julio have suggested. This process of separation is called *distillation*, which, coincidentally, we will study next week.

Do you agree with Mr. Tanaka that the class had learned much, even though they raised many unanswered questions? How much, if anything, has the class learned about distillation as a result of the discussion? Did the students merely learn to attach a name to a process they already knew? Or did they learn something more? How would you characterize Mr. Tanaka's manner during this lesson? Was Mr. Tanaka's teaching strategy a good one? Would it be more efficient to teach about distillation more directly? Why or why not?

Different Learning Styles

The students in Ahmad Ali's sixth-grade class seemed to fall into three groups: those who liked a great deal of teacher attention and guidance, those who worked best independently, and those who fell in between, wanting some guidance but basically self-directed.

Because of this diversity, Ahmad sometimes found it difficult to meet the needs of all his students. This problem was particularly acute for science lessons. Ahmad liked to have his students do experiments and other hands-on science activities. But equipment and materials were limited, so it was usually necessary to divide the class into small groups so that each could work through an experiment while Ahmad engaged the larger groups in other activities. This arrangement did not sit well with the independent workers, nor with those who liked Ahmad's direct guidance, however. But Ahmad justified his plan to himself on the basis of the scarcity of equipment and the need for students to learn to work together. He considered this a necessary social skill. He also believed that doing experiments was a good way to learn science. Thus, he continued the small groups while taking care to be sure each contained a mixture of students with the three learning styles.

Still, he always had nagging doubts. While his students did well in science by and large, Ahmad was not sure he was being fair to the students who really preferred different arrangements. He wondered whether, if he put more thought and energy into the science lessons, he could find a way to deal better with all three learning styles and perhaps integrate different approaches into his teaching.

What would you do? What should decide one's teaching procedures and approach? Is it what students are comfortable with? What materials or equipment are available? What the teacher thinks ought to be done ideally? Is it possible to meet all students' needs? Should the teacher try to do that, or should all students learn to work together? What factors go into decisions about one's approach to teaching in a concrete situation like this?

Compatibility of Approaches

A: In their everyday teaching, teachers ordinarily use a variety of approaches depending on who and what they are teaching. In fact, a teacher might even use a variety of approaches in the same lesson.

B: I might be able to agree with you up to a point. But we need to be careful and not overestimate the compatibility of logically different approaches to teaching. For instance, if one is a liberationist teacher, one would rarely, if ever, act as an executive who dictates the what, when, and how of learning. And a therapist-type teacher certainly wouldn't do that either. Most teachers are quite consistent with their basic approach.

A: But you're talking as if teachers should pick one approach and stick to it no matter what, that to deviate from it would be inconsistent and unfaithful to their basic beliefs. But I'm suggesting that teachers don't need to choose one approach. They should be practical, not idealistic. Practicality calls for matching one's approach to the situation.

B: That's not practicality, that's ducking the issue. "How should I teach?" is the most fundamental professional question a teacher can ask and must answer for himself or herself. You have to care about and believe deeply in why you're doing what you do as a teacher or else you're just acting like a robot responding with built-in external programming to the contingencies of specific situations.

A: But you need not be a robot. A teacher can really believe in the value of each approach and use each intelligently as different situations demand.

B: That sounds good in theory, but I don't think it's possible in practice. It would be like saying one can be a Christian sometimes, a Moslem sometimes, and a Jew sometimes, depending on the spiritual situation. Approaches to teaching are more like religious faiths than like hats you can put on and take off at will. They require a fundamental commitment to deeply believed views about the purpose and value of education in the lives of human beings.

A: Yes, there is that philosophical quality to the calling of teaching, but I still think a good person, a committed teacher, can believe in the use of technical proficiency in aiming both at a student's personal growth and at a depth of knowledge in the traditional subjects without being inconsistent.

B: Perhaps, but not without admitting to a failure to choose to be what one deeply believes in being as an educator.

C: I've been listening to you both and I can't believe what I hear. Choice, approach, religion, philosophy . . . ? Teaching is just a job like any other. You do the best you can, given the social, political, and local realities that you find yourself in. Whatever you might decide or commit yourself to beforehand won't make any difference once you see all the constraints of your job. All this soul searching is just wasted effort. Just learn how to do it and do it. That's all the people want of you.

What do you think? Whose side are you on in this dispute? Why?

Go Fly a Kite

The founder and trustees of Duhey Academy have always believed that competition is an important motivator for learning, as well as a central element in the productive lives of mature persons. Many aspects of school life at Duhey reflect this basic belief. One traditional event that the students really enjoy is a yearly contest held between the sixth grade classes to determine the best product of a class project. This year, the announced project was kite making, but for the first time in the history of the school, no winner could be determined; there was a tie! Mr. Whitehead, the headmaster, and the three seventh-grade teachers who served as judges independently rated both the class 6A and 6C kites equally on each of the points agreed upon. The class 6B kite definitely came off second best, but 6A's and 6C's entries were first-rate in all respects. So the judges declared a draw and awarded the prize, a field trip to the Museum of Manned Flight, to both classes. Mr. Whitehead wondered, though, if the educational experiences leading up to the kites produced were of equal value. Even though both products were equal, maybe the teaching/learning processes of producing them were not. He knew that Mr. Mullins in 6A was a perfectionist. He had heard that, when the project was announced, Mr. Mullins had gone to the library to read everything he could about kites. Then, to the consternation of his wife, he had spent every evening in his study designing and building kites and every weekend testing his models behind the fieldhouse. When he finally developed a model that outperformed all the others, he drew up a set of blueprints and brought them to his class.

Mr. Mullins gave each student materials and a copy of the blueprint, along with careful instructions and teaching demonstrations at each step in the process. He made it clear that this was not only a contest between classes but also within 6A itself. To produce the best kite was the order of the day for each of his students. He would grade them on their effort and on their product. When they had all finished, it turned out that Jim's kite narrowly won out over Karen's, in Mr. Mullins's judgment, even though he gave each an A+. Karen's initial disappointment was softened somewhat when she found out that 6A's entry had won them a tie with 6C and a trip to the museum.

But in 6C Ms. Goody had come at the project quite differently. As soon as she knew what the year's project was to be, she told the class and asked them how they thought they should organize their efforts to win the competition. They all knew that Robert was really good with his hands, so they asked him if he would be "quality control" helper on all the kites they produced. Others volunteered to be designers, color coordinators, supply getters, and fabricators. Before long, five small groups of kite makers formed, with each group working together to produce the best kite they could. Robert put the final touches on each and made them ready for testing outside. The whole class witnessed the tests, and each person rated the kites on the points to be considered by the judges. Ms. Goody tallied the ratings, and 6C's entry was determined and submitted. They were all proud to learn that they had won a trip to the museum.

We haven't mentioned 6B except to say that it lost the contest. That is because Mr. Brayne didn't believe in "fads and frills." Oh, he would see to it that he met the letter of the law, and his class would have a kite for the contest, of course. Each student would be given a homework assignment to make a kite, and then he would draw a name out of the hat to see whose kite would be submitted to represent 6B. That would not take much precious class time, he figured, and so he could continue with the history unit on technology that interestingly enough treated human attempts to overcome the force of gravity through the ages. The students seemed to like the unit. It challenged their minds. Their only regret was that they wouldn't be going to the museum. They thought they would get more out of the trip than those who were going.

Do you think one of these learning experiences was better than the other? Why? What do you think was being learned in each? Imagine yourself as each of the teachers. How would you characterize what is important to do as a teacher if you were Mr. Mullins, Ms. Goody, or Mr. Brayne?

Notes

Chapter 1

1. The emancipationist approach (which we treat briefly in chapter 4) is not represented in our sketches except perhaps obliquely in Roberto's attempt to create a consciousness about cultural differences in his classes. It is an approach that has recently emerged from contemporary neo-Marxist thought, which aims to emancipate ordinary people from the economic and political forces in society that hold them back and keep them from full equality. We have treated this approach in other books in this series. If it is of concern to you, you can read more fully about it there. See Walter Feinberg and Jonas F. Soltis, *School and Society* (New York: Teachers College Press, 1998), and Decker F. Walker and Jonas F. Soltis, *Curriculum and Aims* (New York: Teachers College Press, 1997).

Chapter 2

1. David C. Berliner, "The Executive Functions of Teaching," Instructor, September 1983: 29–39.

2. Michael W. Sedlak, Christopher W. Wheeler, Diana C. Pullin, and Phillip A. Cusick, *Selling Students Short: Classroom Bargains and Academic Reform in the American High School* (New York: Teachers College Press, 1986). See also, Arthur G. Powell, Eleanor Farrar, and David K. Cohen, *The Shopping Mall High School: Winners and Losers in the Educational Marketplace* (Boston: Houghton Mifflin, 1985).

3. David C. Berliner, "What's All the Fuss about Instructional Time?" in Miriam Ben-Peretz and Rainer Bromme, eds., *The Nature of Time in Schools* (New York: Teachers College Press, 1990), pp. 3–35.

4. The best description of this study for the practicing educator is Carolyn Denham and Ann Lieberman, eds., *Time to Learn* (Washington, DC: National Institute of Education, 1980).

5. The relative effectiveness of these elements and their manifestations in teaching practices are examined by Herbert J. Walberg in "Productive Teaching and Instruction: Assessing the Knowledge Base," in Hersholt C. Waxman and Herbert J. Walberg, eds., *Effective Teaching: Current Research* (Berkeley, CA: McCutchan, 1991), pp. 33–62.

6. Thomas L. Good, "Teacher Effectiveness in the Elementary School," *Journal of Teacher Education*, March-April 1979: 53.

7. B. F. Skinner, *The Technology of Teaching* (New York: Appleton-Century-Crofts, 1968), p. 21.

8. Ibid., p. 64.

9. James S. Coleman, E. Campbell, C. Hobson, J. McPartland, A. Mood, and T. York, *Equality of Educational Opportunity* (Washington, DC: U.S. Government Printing Office, 1966).

10. Thomas L. Good, Bruce J. Biddle, and Jere E. Brophy, *Teachers Make a Difference* (New York: Holt, Rinehart and Winston, 1975).

11. Walter Doyle, "Classroom Tasks: The Core of Learning from Teaching," in Michael S. Knapp and Patrick M. Shields, eds., *Better Schooling for the Children of Poverty: Alternatives to Conventional Wisdom* (Berkeley, CA: McCutchan, 1991), p. 237. See also, Walter Doyle, "Classroom Organization and Management," in Merlin C. Wittrock, ed., *Handbook of Research on Teaching*, Third Edition (New York: Macmillan, 1986), pp. 392–431.

Chapter 3

1. This description was provided by Susan Shaw in a personal letter to one of the co-authors and is used here with her permission.

2. Lucy McCormick Calkins, *The Art of Teaching Writing* (Portsmouth, NH: Heinemann, 1986), pp. 3, 5, 6.

3. A. S. Neill, Summerhill (New York: Hart Publishing, 1960).

4. Paul Goodman, *Growing Up Absurd* (New York: Random House, 1956).

5. Paul Goodman, *Compulsory Mis-Education* (New York: Horizon Press, 1964).

6. Paul Goodman, "Freedom and Learning: The Need for Choice," *Saturday Review*, May 18, 1968: 73.

7. Ibid.

8. Ibid.

9. Herbert Kohl, *36 Children* (New York: Signet, New American Library, 1967), pp. 25–26.

10. Abraham Maslow, *Toward a Psychology of Being* (New York: Van Nostrand, 1962).

11. Carl Rogers, *Freedom to Learn* (Columbus, OH: Charles E. Merrill, 1969), p. 103.

12. Ibid., p. 125.

13. Ibid., p. 152.

14. Ibid., p. 153.

15. Ibid.

16. Ibid., p. 108.

17. Nel Noddings and Paul J. Shore, *Awakening the Inner Eye: Intuition in Education* (New York: Teachers College Press, 1984), p. 165.

18. Jean-Paul Sartre, "Existentialism Is a Humanism," in Walter Kaufmann, ed., *Existentialism from Dostoevsky to Sartre* (Cleveland, OH: Meridian/World Publishing, 1956), pp. 290–291.

19. Walter Kaufmann, "Chapter 1: Existentialism from Dostoevsky to Sartre," in Kaufmann, ed., *Existentialism from Dostoevsky to Sartre*, p. 51.

Chapter 4

1. R. S. Peters, "Aims of Education—A Conceptual Inquiry," in R. S. Peters, ed., *The Philosophy of Education* (London: Oxford University Press, 1973), p. 25.

2. Gilbert Ryle, "Can Virtue Be Taught?" in R. F. Dearden, P. H. Hirst, and R. S. Peters, eds., *Education and Reason; Part 3 of Education and the Development of Reason* (London: Routledge & Kegan Paul, 1975), p. 47.

3. Urie Bronfenbrenner, *Two Worlds of Childhood: U.S. and U.S.S.R.* (New York: Simon & Schuster, 1970; Clarion paperback, 1972), quotation from p. 117 of paperback edition.

4. P. H. Hirst, "Liberal Education and the Nature of Knowledge," in Peters, ed., *The Philosophy of Education*, pp. 87–111; also in Dearden, Hirst, and Peters, eds., *Education and Reason: Part 3*, pp. 1–24.

5. Jerome S. Bruner, *The Process of Education* (Cambridge, MA: Harvard University Press, 1960; New York: Random House Vintage Edition, 1963), quotation from p. 71 of the Vintage edition.

6. Ibid. (Vintage edition), pp. 12–13.

7. Paulo Freire, *Pedagogy of the Oppressed* (New York: Herder and Herder, 1970).

8. Ibid., p. 52.

9. Ibid., p. 66.

10. See, for example, Michael Apple, *Teachers and Texts: A Political Economy of Class and Gender Relations* (New York: Routledge, Chapman and Hall, 1988); Stanley Aronowitz and Henry A. Giroux, *Education under Siege; The Conservative, Liberal and Radical Debate over Schooling* (South Hadley, MA: Bergin and Garvey, 1985); Peter McClaren, *Life in Schools: An Introduction to Critical Pedagogy in the Foundations of Education* (New York: Longman, 1989); Thomas S. Popkewitz, *A Political Sociology of Educational Reform: Power/ Knowledge in Teaching, Teacher Education, and Research* (New York: Teachers College Press, 1991); and Ira Shor, *Critical Teaching and Everyday Life* (Chicago: University of Chicago Press, 1987; originally published in 1980).

11. National Commission on Excellence in Education, *A Nation at Risk: The Imperative for Educational Reform* (Washington, DC: U.S. Government Printing Office, 1983).

12. Mortimer J, Adler, *The Paideia Proposal: An Educational Manifesto* (New York: Macmillan, 1982), pp. 19–20.

13. Ibid., p. 20.

14. Jane Roland Martin, "Needed: A New Paradigm for Liberal Education," in Jonas F. Soltis, ed., *Philosophy and Education: Eightieth Yearbook of the National Society for the Study of Education* (Chicago: University of Chicago Press, 1981), p. 44.

Chapter 5

1. Harry S. Broudy, *The Real World of Public Schools* (New York: Harcourt Brace Jovanovich, 1972), p. 82.

2. For a more detailed exposition of the idea of the liberationist approach being more fundamental, see Jonas F. Soltis, "The Virtues of Teaching," *Journal of Thought*, Fall 1987: 61–67.

Chapter 6

1. Kieran Egan, *The Educated Mind* (Chicago: University of Chicago, 1997).

2. For helpful background information on constructivism, consult Denis C. Phillips, "The Good, The Bad, and the Ugly: The Many Faces of Constructivism," *Education Researcher*, 24(7), October 1995: 5–12; Virginia Richardson, *Constructivist Teacher Education* (London: Falmer Press, 1997); Virginia Richardson, "Teacher Education and the Construction of Meaning," in Gary A. Griffin, ed., *Teacher Education for a New Century* (Yearbook of the National Society for Education; Chicago: University of Chicago Press, in press); also a special issue of *Educational Researcher*, 23(7), October 1994, devoted to the topic of constructivism.

3. On our reading of Richardson (cited above), she agrees that a teacher could hold a constructivist view of learning while adopting an executive approach to teaching.

4. Lawrence Blum, *Moral Perception and Particularity* (New York: Cambridge University Press, 1994); Carol Gilligan, *In a Different Voice* (Cambridge, MA: Harvard University Press, 1982, 1993); Donna H. Kerr, *Beyond Education: In Search of Nurture* (Work in Progress Series, No. 2; Seattle, WA: Institute for Educational Inquiry, 1993); Nel Noddings, *Caring* (Berkeley, CA: University of California Press, 1984), and *The Challenge to Care in Schools* (New York: Teachers College Press, 1992).

5. Annette C. Baier, *Moral Prejudices* (Cambridge, MA: Harvard University Press, 1994); John I. Goodlad, *Educational Renewal* (San Francisco: Jossey-Bass, 1994); Jane Roland Martin, *The Schoolhome* (Cambridge, MA: Harvard University Press, 1992).

6. Donna Kerr, "Voicing Democracy in an Imperfect World," in Wilma Smith & Gary D Fenstermacher, eds., *Fostering Leadership for Educational Renewal* (San Francisco, CA: Jossey-Bass, in press).

7. Early proponents of this view of the purpose of education were R. S. Peters, *Education as Initiation* (London: Evans Bros., Ltd., 1964), and .Paul Hirst, *Knowledge and the Curriculum* (London: Routledge and Kegan Paul, 1974).

8. This point is thoughtfully developed in Jennifer M. Gore, *The Struggle for Pedagogies* (New York: Routledge, 1993).

9. Ira Shore, *Empowering Education* (Chicago: University of Chicago Press, 1992).

10. Patricia H. Hinchey, *Finding Freedom in the Classroom: A Practical Introduction to Critical Theory* (New York: Peter Lang Publishing, 1998); Joan Wink, *Critical Pedagogy* (New York: Longman, 1997).

11. Paulo Freire, *Pedagogy of the Oppressed* (New Revised 20th Anniversary Edition). New York: Continuum Press, 1993.

12. Michael Oakeshott, "A Place of Learning," in T. Fuller, ed., *The Voice of Liberal Learning*, (New Haven, CT: Yale University Press, 1989, p. 38.

13. Parker J. Palmer, *The Courage to Teach* (San Francisco: Jossey-Bass, 1998).

Bibliographic Essay

The Executive Approach

The notion of the executive functions of teaching was developed by David C. Berliner, who directed the ground-breaking study of teaching known as the Beginning Teacher Evaluation Study. The best description of this study for the practitioner is still a government-sponsored book edited by Carolyn Denham and Ann Lieberman, entitled *Time to Learn* (Washington, DC: National Institute of Education, 1980). Berliner's most recent summary of what has been learned from studies of instructional time, "What's All the Fuss about Instructional Time?", may be found in *The Nature of Time in Schools*, edited by Miriam Ben-Peretz and Rainer Bromme (New York: Teachers College Press, 1990).

The research program that undergirds much of the executive approach is remarkably well defended in two publications by a scholar often referred to as the father of research on teaching, N. L. Gage: *The Scientific Basis of the Art of Teaching* (New York: Teachers College Press, 1978) and *Hard Gains in the Soft Sciences* (Bloomington, IN: Phi Delta Kappa, 1985). A sense of the controversy that has surrounded the process-product design may be gained from another piece by Gage and Margaret C. Needels, "Process-Product Research on Teaching: A Review of the Criticisms," *The Elementary School Journal*, 89(3), 1989: 253–300. An update on this analysis may be found in Margaret C. Needels and N. L. Gage, "Essence and Accident in Process-Product Research on Teaching," in Hersholt C. Waxman and Herbert J. Walberg, eds., *Effective Teaching: Current Research* (Berkeley, CA: McCutchan, 1991). Gage's students and close colleagues have produced an excellent anthology in his honor entitled *Talks to Teachers* (New York: Random House, 1987). It is edited by David Berliner and Barak Rosenschine. Nearly all the articles are accessible to the general reader.

The work of researchers on teaching, embracing many different research designs, is readily available in a number of recent works. One frequently used by students of research on teaching is the *Handbook of Research on Teaching*, Third Edition, edited by Merlin C. Wittrock (New York: Macmillan,

1986). Although many of the articles are technical, this is a work with which all teachers should be acquainted. The essays in *Knowledge Base for the Beginning Teacher*, edited by Maynard C. Reynolds (Oxford, UK: Pergamon Press, 1989), are somewhat more accessible to the new professional but are not as complete or as focused as those in the *Handbook of Research on Teaching*. Another helpful work is the Waxman and Walberg anthology, *Effective Teaching* (see above).

The imaginative work of Walter Doyle is available only in journal articles and anthologies. The reader is directed to Doyle's article in the *Handbook of Research on Teaching* (see above); to his foundational piece "Academic Work," *Review of Educational Research*, 53, 1983: 159–199; and to his analysis of how the structuring of academic tasks affects the disadvantaged learner, "Classroom Tasks: The Core of Learning from Teaching," in Michael S. Knapp and Patrick M. Shields, eds., *Better Schooling for the Children of Poverty: Alternatives to Conventional Wisdom* (Berkeley, CA: McCutchan, 1991).

How research on teaching has influenced teaching practices, particularly in forming an executive approach to teaching, is dramatically evident in the second edition of the general teaching methods text *Learning to Teach*, by Richard Arends (New York: McGraw-Hill, 1991). This text, perhaps more than any other general teaching methods text, is based on the knowledge and understanding accumulated over the last twenty years of teaching research. It is interesting that Arends, following Berliner, entitles one of three major sections of the book "The Executive Functions of Teaching." Two other useful works in this same tradition are Gary D. Borich, *Observation Skills for Effective Teaching* (Columbus, OH: Merrill Publishing Company, 1990); and Thomas L. Good and Jere E. Brophy, *Looking in Classrooms*, Fourth Edition (New York: Harper & Row, 1987).

The Therapist Approach

Recent work exemplifying the therapist approach is not abundant. The educational reform movements of the 1980s called for a return to the basics, accountability, national assessments, and the beginnings of a national curriculum. Concern about individual persons, their personal growth and authenticity, gave way to the perceived need to prepare productive workers for the economic competition between nations.

One beacon in this void has been the work of Nel Noddings. Her book *Caring: A Feminine Approach to Ethics and Moral Education* (Berkeley, CA: University of California Press, 1984) has now been followed by *The Challenge to Care in Schools* (New York: Teachers College Press, 1992). She argues that schools seem only to care about the math and verbal aptitudes and achievements of children, not about them as children and young adults who have other multiple and unique talents. Her vision of a caring school with a curriculum that teaches care for self, others, nature, human artifacts, instruments, and ideas is a radical, yet compelling one for the therapist-oriented educator.

Other contemporary therapist-oriented literature is also available. We have already alluded to the way teachers of English and advocates of writing across the curriculum recently have seized on the device of journal writing to engage individual students in authentically reflecting on their own beliefs and personhood. Lucy Caulkins's *The Art of Teaching Writing* (Portsmouth, NH: Heinemann, 1986) is a good introduction to this idea. A broad approach to the idea of a therapist-oriented middle and high school curriculum is provided by James A. Beane and Richard P. Lipka in *Self-Concept, Self-Esteem and the Curriculum* (New York: Teachers College Press, 1986). Claire V. Korn documents the work of seven actual schools operating in the therapist tradition in her *Alternative American Schools* (Albany: State University of New York Press, 1991). A reflective view of how a teacher can develop sensitivity toward individual students can be found in Max van Manen's *The Tact of Teaching: The Meaning of Pedagogical Thoughtfulness* (Albany: State University of New York Press, 1991). And finally, *Stories Lives Tell* (New York: Teachers College Press, 1991), edited by Carol Witherwell and Nel Noddings, is rich with life histories and stories of teachers who believe that education means taking seriously both the quest for life's meaning and the call to care for persons.

While the concern with each child's own growth and development is an old one dating back at least to Jean Jacques Rousseau (1717–1778) and his famous book *Emile* (London: J. M. Dent and Sons, 1911), it is also a major theme in the child-centered progressive education movement in the late nineteenth and early twentieth centuries. Lawrence A. Cremin's classic history of that movement, *The Transformation of the Schools* (New York: Vintage Books, 1961), provides an excellent overview.

If you have an interest in the more recent history of the therapist approach, the so-called popular reform books of the 1960s are fascinating to read and extremely provocative. Among the best in education are the following: George Dennison, *The Lives of Children* (New York: Vintage/Random House, 1969); Jonathan Kozol, Death at an Early Age (New York: Houghton Mifflin, 1967); Ivan Illich, *Deschooling Society* (New York: Harper & Row, 1970); A. S. Neill, *Summerhill* (New York: Hart Publishing, 1960); and Everett Reimer, *School Is Dead* (Garden City, NY: Doubleday/Anchor, 1971). The work of Paul Goodman is, of course, now classic. *Growing Up Absurd* was published by Random House in 1956. The Goodman quotations in chapter 3 were taken from an excellent short piece called "Freedom and Learning: The Need for Choice," which he wrote for the *Saturday Review* (May 18, 1968, pp. 73–75).

There are also many works on the emergence of humanistic psychology. One of the best introductions for the beginner is a short anthology edited by Floyd W. Matson, *Without/Within: Behaviorism and Humanism* (Belmont, CA: Wadsworth, 1973). There is no reason to avoid the original works, however. They are well written and filled with appealing ideas. See especially these pivotal works: Carl R. Rogers, *Freedom to Learn* (Columbus, OH: Charles E. Merrill, 1969); and Carl R. Rogers, ed., *Freedom to Learn for the 80's* (Columbus, OH: Charles E. Merrill, 1980). Also vitally important are Gordon W. Allport, *Becoming* (New Haven, CT: Yale University Press, 1955); and Abraham H. Maslow, *Toward a Psychology of Being* (New York: Van Nostrand, 1962).

It is somewhat more difficult to recommend works on existentialism to the beginning teacher. There are different types of existentialists—literary, philosophical, religious—and none of them wrote very directly about education. Perhaps the most accessible general introduction for teachers still would be David Denton, ed., *Existentialism and Phenomenology in Education* (New York: Teachers College Press, 1974). If you wish to get a sense of what an existential commitment means in teaching, one of the best works you can read is Maxine Greene's *Teacher as Stranger* (Belmont, CA: Wadsworth, 1973). Existentialist writing is generally not easy to follow. It sometimes helps to become familiar with several different views before becoming deeply enmeshed in a particular version or writer. The edited selections in Walter Kaufmann's *Existentialism from Dostoevsky to Sartre* (Cleveland, OH: Meridian/World Publishing, 1956) still provides one of the best introductions to the writings of classical existentialist thinkers.

The Liberationist Approach

There is an enormous literature on what we have called the liberationist approach to teaching, primarily because this approach has deep historical roots and is so closely connected to philosophical ideas. Any text that spans the history of educational thought from ancient to modern times will suggest a host of important sources to read. One that we find ourselves turning to again and again is Kingsley Price, *Education and Philosophical Thought*, Second Edition (Boston: Allyn & Bacon, 1967). As for some of the more recent work, it may be helpful to begin with Bruce A. Kimball, *Orators and Philosophers: A History of the Idea of Liberal Education* (New York: Teachers College Press, 1986). Most frequently, liberal education is taken to be the work of colleges, but as we have seen, Mortimer J. Adler's *The Paideia Proposal: An Educational Manifesto* (New York: Macmillan, 1982), which was discussed in chapter 4, is a brief, highly readable argument for liberal education in today's secondary schools.

As the reader enters the more strictly philosophical literature, the complexity increases a bit, but so does the depth of understanding. The work of the British philosophers R. S. Peters and P. H. Hirst is widely available. Two key sources of their writing are identified in the notes to chapter 4. The idea of liberal education as the development of mind through initiation into the forms of knowledge has been the major theme of Hirst's philosophical work, and a collection of his major papers is worth a visit for those who want to explore this idea in depth, see Paul H. Hirst, *Knowledge and the Curriculum* (London: Routledge & Kegan Paul, 1974). Another excellent treatment of liberationist theory is John Passmore, *The Philosophy of Teaching* (Cambridge, MA: Harvard University Press, 1980). Passmore attempts to explicate the emotional aspects of the liberationist approach with the same intensity as the knowledge aspects. Several American philosophers of education have propounded related views but with significant adaptations. One of these is D. Bob Gowin, whose *Educating* (Ithaca, NY: Cornell University Press, 1981) focuses attention on teaching in all subjects for meaning and understanding. Israel Scheffler, in his long career at Harvard, has explored many themes relevant to liberationist thought. Two such works are his *Reason and Teaching* (New York: Routledge & Kegan Paul, 1973) and *Of Human Potential* (New York: Routledge & Kegan Paul, 1985). His student Harvey Siegel also has added to the liberationist view of education with his extensive analysis of teaching for critical thinking in *Educating Reason* (New York: Routledge, 1991).

On the potentially harmful consequences of certain forms of liberal education, Allan Bloom's popular *The Closing of the American Mind: How Higher Education Has Failed Democracy and Impoverished the Souls of Today's Students* (New York: Simon & Shuster, 1987) provides a most interesting example. Bloom takes the Greco-Roman notion of *paideia* so seriously and so single-mindedly that he practically makes the case for the therapist and emancipationist in their critiques of liberal education. E. D. Hirsch's *Cultural Literacy: What Every American Needs to Know* (Boston: Houghton Mifflin, 1987) errs on the other side by concluding that a list of shared cultural facts constitutes the essence of a liberal education.

As is evident from our discussion of the liberationist approach to teaching, moral and ethical considerations also are a prominent part of this approach. These considerations are discussed in depth, but in a manner accessible to the lay reader, in *The Moral Dimensions of Teaching*, edited by John I. Goodlad, Roger Soder, and Kenneth A. Sirotnik (San Francisco: Jossey-Bass, 1990), and in other books in this series; see Kenneth Strike and Jonas Soltis, *The Ethics of Teaching*, Third Edition (New York: Teachers College Press, 1998) and Decker Walker and Jonas Soltis, *Curriculum and Aims*, Third Edition (New York: Teachers College Press, 1997).

Suggestions for General Reading

A central purpose of this book is to encourage you to reflect carefully on the purposes of education, as well as how your approach to teaching embodies your sense of these purposes. You can accomplish these goals by reading the works cited above, but each of them clearly reflects an orientation to one of the three approaches, else it would not be mentioned there. It is also helpful to read more generally on the topic of teaching, especially works that describe the efforts of others to work through the nature of teaching.

An excellent anthology, representing a broad range of perspectives as well as covering the gamut from school teacher to teaching researcher, is *Teachers, Teaching, & Teacher Education*, edited by Margo Okazawa-Rey, James Anderson, and Rob Traver (Reprint Series No. 19, *Harvard Educational Review*, 1987). This work collects thirty-four articles from prior issues of the *Harvard Educational Review*, which, taken together, represent an excellent set of readings on the topic of teaching. While on the subject of the *Harvard Educational Review*, it is one of the premier journals in the field of education. Two other outstanding generalist journals are the *American Journal of Education* (University of Chicago) and *Teachers College Record* (Teachers College, Columbia University). The *Phi Delta Kappan* and *Educational Leadership* magazines also offer much that is relevant, although in somewhat more popular a fashion and format than the three journals just mentioned.

Another anthology of value, also including a wide range of authors writing thoughtfully on the topic of teaching, is *What Teachers Need to Know: The Knowledge, Skills, and Values Essential to Good Teaching*, by David D. Dill and Associates (San Francisco: Jossey-Bass, 1990). Turning to works by a single author, Philip W. Jackson has long written with clarity and insight on teaching. His latest work on this topic is entitled *The Practice of Teaching* (New York: Teachers College Press, 1986). A scholar-practitioner of long standing, Vito Perrone of Harvard University also offers an absorbing series of reflections on teaching; *A Letter to Teachers* was published in 1991 by Jossey-Bass (San Francisco).

The second edition of this book is being completed during the presidency of George Bush, who frequently indicates he would like to be known as the education president. Though little of substance has yet occurred, there is much talk of reform and restructuring. Two books of value in developing an insight into educational reform, particularly as these reforms impact on teaching, are *Schools for the Twenty-First Century*, by Phillip S. Schlechty (San Francisco: Jossey-Bass, 1990); and *The Predictable Failure of Educational Reform*, by Seymour B. Sarason (San Francisco: Jossey-Bass, 1990). Finally, we encourage you to read *Among Schoolchildren* by Tracy Kidder (Boston: Houghton Mifflin, 1989). This best-selling work offers an excellent opportunity to "see" a teacher and her students through the eye of an astute observer.

You will find it a fine companion to both this book and the other works mentioned in this section.

Additional Selections for the Third Edition

In almost every case, the books recommended in previous sections of this Bibliographic Essay continue to be excellent choices for further pursuit of a specific topic. A few books are out of print, such as the Okazawa-Ray, Anderson, and Traver book mentioned in the immediately preceding section, but these are the exception, not the rule. You should have little difficulty finding these books or periodicals in a college or university library, and quite a few of the books cited here will be available in a well-stocked public library. In this updated section, we will continue to mention only works we think will hold the interest of the aspiring teacher and are likely to be accessible to the majority of our readers.

On the Executive Approach. For a clear picture of how an executive notion of competence shapes the way schooling ought to take place, see Richard J. Murnane and Frank Levy, *Teaching the New Basic Skills* (New York: Martin Kessler Books, The Free Press, 1996). An argument for competence, with flourishes of classical liberation, is forcefully set forth in Linda Darling-Hammond's *The Right to Learn* (San Francisco: Jossey-Bass, 1997). A rather startling analysis of educational data, showing that schools have done far better at the cultivation of competence than many critics of public education would have us believe is David C. Berliner's and Bruce J. Biddle's *The Manufactured Crisis* (Reading, MA: Addison-Wesley, 1995). Yes, this is the same David Berliner who figures so prominently in the development of the Executive Approach in chapter 2.

On the Fostering Approach. The literature on fostering is not easily brought to hand, for as you may recall, we "created" this approach from a fairly broad spectrum of literature. The work by Nel Noddings, noted previously in the Therapist Approach section of this essay, continues to provide an excellent foundation for fostering. Work by Donna Kerr on nurture is just beginning to emerge; see note 6 to chapter 6, as well as her essay, "Toward a Democratic Rhetoric of Schooling," in John I. Goodlad and Timothy J. McMannon, eds., *The Public Purpose of Education and Schooling* (San Francisco: Jossey-Bass, 1997). Another work mentioned in the citations to chapter 6 and worth mentioning again is Jane Roland Martin's *The Schoolhome* (Cambridge, MA: Harvard University Press, 1992). Drawing us into the intersections between John Dewey and Maria Montessori, Martin makes a powerful argument for why the school should model the home in its emphasis on love and relationship. Herbert Kohl is a writer who often blurs the distinction between fostering and critical liberation. One of his latest books, *I Won't Learn From You* (New York: The New Press, W. W. Norton, 1994), turns the reader's mind upside down in the most delightful ways. It is a treat to read.

On the Classical Liberation Approach. Mortimer Adler and E. D. Hirsch continue to serve as vital proponents for the classical liberationist position. More eclectic in approach, and more gentle in tone, John I. Goodlad's latest work, *In Praise of Education* (New York: Teachers College Press, 1997) offers a number of important insights into classical liberation. Among those who argue for the restoration of classical liberation, in the manner of the Western Canon, are Harold Bloom, *The Western Canon* (New York: Harcourt Brace & Company, 1994), and Andrew Delbanco, *Required Reading* (New York: Farrar, Straus and Giroux, 1997). A delightful excursion into the classical literature is provided by David Denby in *Great Books* (New York: Simon & Schuster, 1996). Denby is a film critic who in mid-life returns to Columbia University to retake the well-known, required courses in Western Civilization. For a passionate and articulate defense of classical liberalism against its detractors, including critical liberation, see Harvey Siegel, *Rationality Redeemed* (New York: Routledge, 1997). Among the strident voices arguing for a narrowly defined version of classical liberation is Lynne V. Cheney, *Telling the Truth* (New York: Simon & Schuster, 1995). You can gain a sense of Cheney's "take" on contemporary schooling from the subtitle of this book, "Why Our Culture and Our Country Have Stopped Making Sense—and What We Can Do About It." A different kind of work is James W. Loewen's *Lies My Teacher Told Me* (New York: The New Press, W. W. Norton, 1995), which details how U.S. history is so often incorrectly taught in our schools. It is a wonderful primer in how conceptions of what we know impact curriculum and instruction, and it also serves as a valuable insight into how race and culture are treated in many U.S. histories.

On the Critical Liberation Approach. In the context of critical liberation, readers may want to look the new edition of Paulo Freire's classic, *Pedagogy of the Oppressed*, which is cited in note 11 for chapter 6. In addition, Freire has also written a helpful companion work entitled *Education for Critical Consciousness* (New York: Continuum, 1993). Additional resources that explore the key ideas of critical pedagogy are Peter McLaren, *Life in Schools* (2nd ed., New York: Longman, 1994), and Ira Shor's *Critical Teaching and Everyday Life* (Chicago: University of Chicago Press, 1980, 1987). Yet another useful book setting forth the main lines of critical thought in education is Michael Apple's *Cultural Politics and Education* (New York: Teachers College Press, 1996). In the notes to chapter 6 we cited a number of works we thought offered the most concise guidance to teachers interested in critical liberation;

as a reminder, we mention them once again as excellent sources of help: Patricia H. Hinchey, *Finding Freedom in the Classroom: A Practical Introduction to Critical Theory* (NY: Peter Lang Publishing, 1998); Ira Shor, *Empowering Education* (Chicago: University of Chicago Press, 1992); and Joan Wink, *Critical Pedagogy* (New York: Longman, Addison-Wesley, 1997).

Multiculturalism. There are quite a few books available on multicultural education. Students with whom we have worked have found those by James A. Banks very helpful, particularly *An Introduction to Multicultural Education* (Boston: Allyn and Bacon, 1994). Also helpful as an introduction to the topic is Thomas J. La Belle and Christopher R. Ward, *Multiculturalism and Education* (Albany, NY: State University of New York Press, 1994). For insight into the intersections of multiculturalism and critical liberation, consult Christine E. Sleeter and Peter L. McLaren, eds., *Multicultural Education, Critical Pedagogy, and the Politics of Difference* (Albany, NY: State University of New York Press, 1995). The politics of multicultural education are explored by Catherine Cornbleth and Dexter Waugh in *The Great Speckled Bird* (New York: St. Martin's Press, 1995), who use case studies of curriculum reform and textbook adoption in California and New York to illustrate how policy decisions about education are made. A provocative work, in a more theoretical vein (but highly informative) is K. Anthony Appiah and Amy Gutmann, *Color Conscious* (Princeton: Princeton University Press, 1996).

General Reading. Among the outstanding general reading that expands on ideas developed in this book, we recommend, with considerable enthusiasm, Neil Postman's *The End of Education* (New York: Vintage, Random House, 1995). Jonathan Kozol's superb studies of schooling and poverty are must-reading for all educators, and include *Savage Inequalities* (New York: Crown, Harper Perennial, 1991) and the follow-up piece, *Amazing Grace* (New York: Crown, 1995). In chapter 6 we referred to Parker J. Palmer's *The Courage to Teach* (San Francisco: Jossey-Bass, 1998), and want to remind you that it is a worthwhile book. Finally, for an upbeat and inspiring depiction of what goes on in America's classrooms, see Mike Rose, *Possible Lives* (Houghton Mifflin, Penguin, 1995). As we did in previous editions, we encourage you to keep abreast of educational ideas by attending to the relevant periodical literature, including the education newspaper, *Education Week*, and the monthly magazines, *Phi Delta Kappan* and *Educational Leadership*.